D1261300

Anti-Nazi Writers in Exile

Egbert Krispyn

Anti-Nazi Writers
in Exile

The University of Georgia Press
Athens

Copyright © 1978 by the University of Georgia Press
Athens 30602

Set in 11 on 12 point Mergenthaler Garamond
Printed in the United States of America

Library of Congress Cataloging in Publication Data

Krispyn, Egbert.
    Anti-Nazi writers in exile.
    Bibliography.
    Includes index.
    1. German literature—20th century—History and
criticism.   2. German literature in foreign countries—
History and criticism.   3. National socialism in literature.
4. Anti-Nazi movement.   5. Germany—History—
1933– 1945.   I. Title.
PT405.K748   830'.9   77-9568
ISBN 0-8203-0430-1

"In the emigration he played on a stone fiddle . . ."
                                    Leonhard Frank

Contents

Introduction

The Second World War and Hitler's Third Reich lie far enough
behind us to have become history. We can now focus sharply and
dispassionately on the events of the thirties and forties, without
the blurring that results from a lack of emotional or temporal distance. At the same time there has in recent years been a tremendous upsurge of general interest in the Nazi era. A steady stream
of books, films, and television programs dealing with its various
episodes and personalities bears witness to the public's fascination
with this topic. No doubt an element of superficial sensational-
ism enters into this preoccupation, but there is a more serious
basis for it as well.

In Nazism the nationalistic currents of the preceding century
reached their peak of fanaticism and aggressiveness. The Hitler
regime also marked the full-scale outbreak of modern absolutism
in the form of a dictatorship based on demagogy and terror. The
Second World War furthermore resulted in a quantum leap in the
development of military strategy and equipment, including guer-
rilla warfare, jet planes, and nuclear bombs. In many ways the
Nazi era therefore stands at the origin of trends that dominate
life in the second half of the twentieth century. The fascination
with the history of the thirties and forties is from this viewpoint
a sign of widespread concern with many features of the present
age. Their fascist nature is in many instances only too obvious. In
this sense the large amount of exposure given to this topic in the
different media may result in making the public more aware of

the roots of many present-day problems. The Nazi story reveals the threats posed by the fascist heritage to the traditional ways of life.

In all the publicity on the subject, generally little attention has so far been given to the emigration as one of the period's most revealing aspects. This neglect is due to the nature of the topic. The emigrants were too diverse and at the same time too amorphous a group to be dealt with effectively. Many of them were driven out of Germany simply on racial grounds and were not interested or involved in politics either before or after they went into exile. Moreover for the overwhelming majority the expulsion from their native soil was final—the experience was so traumatic that they were no longer interested in the German-speaking world and had no desire ever to return there. All they wanted was to settle down and build a new life in another country and become assimilated with its population as soon as possible.

But there was a special group of exiles who, while sharing the general fate of emigration with all others deemed undesirable by Hitler, stood out from the rest in several respects. The writers were on the whole politically conscious and often actively engaged in public life. They were almost all in their literary activity so attuned to central European life and especially to the German language that on those grounds alone they were vitally interested in Germany's fate and future. Only Hitler's defeat would enable them to return. And, in addition, as writers they left extensive records of their experiences, fears, hopes, and aspirations. In spite of all their individual differences, the exile authors as a group therefore have a much more clearly defined profile than the emigrants in general.

The story of the literary emigration provides one of the most effective focal points for an understanding and assessment of the Hitler years. It is further significant that the antifascist exile writers were the only segment of the population that from the beginning consistently resisted the Nazis. This group proved with very few exceptions to be immune to their threats and violence as well as to their blandishments. From most viewpoints the Nazis tend to appear as the embodiment of some kind of incontrovertible fate. In the descriptions and dramatizations of death camp atrocities, for instance, the defenselessness and passivity of the victims inevitably cause their tormentors to be demonized. They seem to represent some supernatural principle of evil and are therefore removed from the sphere of human legal, moral, and ethical responsibilities. The exile writers adamantly refused to be silenced and so provoked the Nazis to abusive and vengeful reactions. Their misdeeds were thus shown to be the work of men, and the evil they perpetrated appeared as the product of warped minds and derailed societies.

Whereas in retrospect it is a distinct achievement of the literary emigration to have brought out this facet of the Nazi regime, this was not at the time one of its conscious objectives. The exile writers strove for a more directly and immediately effective opposition against the fascists with the aim of restoring normal, free literary and cultural life to the German realm as soon as possible after the defeat of Hitler. To achieve these ends, up until the outbreak of the war they devoted themselves largely to enlightening the public outside Hitler's realm about the reality of the Nazi regime and the threat it posed to the rest of the world. At the same time they also laid claim to being the representatives of the true spiritual and cultural values of their people, values that were suppressed and betrayed by Germany's new rulers.

For the majority of the exiled authors their banishment was a period of material misery. Yet the hardships of physical existence paled in comparison with the disappointments and frustrations of their literary pursuits and their activities as publicists. All their self-sacrifice and all their dedication to the cause of antifascism were basically futile. They succeeded neither in alerting the world about Hitler's true nature and intentions before it was too late nor in revitalizing Germany's humanistic and literary heritage after the Third Reich had collapsed. Their stand against totalitarianism was admirable and the courage of their convictions often impressive, but in the final analysis Leonhard Frank was right in his bitterly disillusioned assessment that they had failed to influence the course of the world with their words—that they had played on a fiddle of stone.

Still, even if they did not achieve their immediate objectives, in a historical perspective the literary emigration appears as an integral part of the great upheaval that forever changed the world in which we live. And the experiences of the exile writers not only provide an often moving human document and a revealing reflection on the fascists' practices in dealing with their most persistent and vocal adversaries; to a large extent the story of the emigration is also an account of the varying mixtures of generosity, hypocrisy, and callousness with which the Allied countries treated those of Hitler's victims who got away. In retrospect the literary opposition against Hitler looms large against the turbulent horizon of the thirties and forties. If it was a fiasco in its own historical framework, with the passing years it has assumed the proportions of a monument. It honors those who sacrificed themselves as men and artists in a desperate battle against evil, and it serves to warn of the terrible frailty of the spirit in a world ruled by the laws of the jungle.

Literary scholars, historians, and political scientists have amassed many facts and figures about specific phases and personalities of the literary emigration, but so far no attempt has been made to present a coherent picture of this most revealing and interesting facet of the Hitler era. This volume presents such an overview, which may serve as a useful frame of reference for the study of specific topics in exile literature, while at the same time filling a gap in the more general coverage of the history of the Nazi years. A survey of this nature is of course largely derivative, being based on previous research on the subject by a large number of scholars and on eyewitness accounts by some of those involved. This book therefore does not claim or intend to make an original contribution to scholarship, except in the interpretive synthesis that underlies the presentation as a whole. Under these circumstances it seems justified and in the interest of readability desirable to limit source references and annotation to the more controversial issues and judgments. In all other cases the interested reader will be better served by the appended bibliography, which in citing all the works consulted in compiling this account provides an extensive, although by no means exhaustive, reading list.

Anti-Nazi Writers in Exile

I:
1933–1939

1
Background

Exile is a basic human experience—so much so that Adam and Eve as outcasts from Paradise are symbols of mankind's beginnings. Among those who since then have been forced to leave their homes and face the dangers and difficulties of life in a strange country there have been many writers. From Ovid to Hugo, from Dante to Bunin, men of letters who incurred the wrath of their rulers have had to flee their native soil. The German realm has always contributed its share—and often more than that—to the world's crop of exiled authors. The medieval courtly poet Walther von der Vogelweide; Ulrich von Hutten, political and religious pamphleteer of the Reformation era; and the idealistic dramatist and historian Schiller in the eighteenth century are but some of the most illustrious names that come to mind.

But hard and bitter though the experiences of the emigrants in those earlier days often were, they remained individual cases until Chancellor Metternich in the first half of the nineteenth century introduced a new dimension of hardship into the exiled writers' fate. He tried to repress the political shockwaves of nationalism in post-Napoleonic Europe by outlawing the progressive writers collectively. A decree of the Federal Diet of 1835 accused a liberal group of literati known as the Young Germans of attacking the Christian religion in the most impertinent manner, thereby calling in question the existing social conditions and destroying all discipline and morality. The publication of their writings was to be prevented. To that end repressive laws and police ordinances were to be applied relentlessly against them and all those who printed, published, or distributed their works.

As a result of this decree many literary careers were ruined; some writers suffered imprisonment and even death, while others were forced to live abroad in poverty and misery. But the lack of political unity among the thirty-nine sovereign states that formed the German Federation and the limited duration of the repressive rule which was repealed in 1842 saved many of the Young Germans from the worst. And beside those who were hard hit by the decree there were also cases like that of the prominent publicist Heinrich Laube, who in 1835 was sentenced to seven years imprisonment. He was released after spending a comfortable year and a half as the house guest, or more accurately the castle guest, of Prince Pückler.

A hundred years later under the Nazis the persecution of the literary opposition was much more consistent and relentless. But under Metternich as under Hitler entire groups were involved rather than individuals, and draconic measures were taken to keep their works out of the hands of the people. Such similarities indicate that the Nazi terror did not descend on Germany out of a clear blue sky. Age-old traditions of an absolutism that deprived its subjects of all political influence and power had molded the civic character of the Germans. Many aspects of National Socialism appear as distorted, extreme manifestations of this ingrained spirit.

Specific historical circumstances did much to turn the traditional subservient streak of the German people into a mental attitude that the fascists could exploit to their own ends. For nearly a century after the French Revolution, Germany continued to be split up in a large number of small, jealously autonomous principalities. Under their autocratic rulers the Germans were unable to follow the lead of their western neighbors in ridding themselves of outworn feudalistic political structures. Because they could not gain national unification and centralization the Germans perverted the lessons of the Revolution, turning them into a romantic-mystic notion of ethnic uniqueness which was not bound by borders.

In the turbulent years around the middle of the nineteenth

century there actually was much revolutionary fervor in the German realm, but all attempts to overthrow the establishment by force failed. This disappointment of all liberal, progressive ambitions to catch up with the rest of Europe in terms of democratization caused a widespread mood of resignation and disillusionment. Under these circumstances the people let themselves be taken in by Chancellor Bismarck's phony scheme of a conservative-nationalistic "revolution from above," which was imposed on the country under the revealing motto of "outward unity before internal liberty."

Even so, the fact that the Germans were accustomed to unconditional obedience to those in power does not in itself account for the emergence of Hitler's fascist dictatorship. The developments in Germany formed part of a general upsurge of totalitarianism in many western countries in the early part of the twentieth century. From the Marxist point of view the rise to power of dictatorial rightist regimes in Italy and Spain, for instance, and related political trends in other countries appeared as a last desperate attempt by the doomed capitalist system to defend itself against the inexorable advance of Communism. To the less dogmatic mind the role of fascism as a lower middle-class movement in the service of the established power structure was only one aspect of a highly complex historical process.

Since the first half of the eighteenth century, under the ever increasing impact of the industrialization of the western world drastic political, social, and economic chages had taken place. As the modern technological world evolved, new ways of life gradually eroded the individualism which since the end of the Middle Ages had set the tone of European thinking. As the people flocked to the rapidly growing cities with their factories and businesses, the old clanlike, patriarchal families broke down and gave way to the modern, small, impermanent consumer units consisting of a set of parents with their young children. As a result people no longer felt themselves part of a family tradition from which they derived a sense of pride and identity. They were at the mercy of trends and fashions manipulated at will by the new economic overlords, and they thus became part of a faceless mass. The rise of aggressive nationalism further helped to reduce the individual human being to an anonymous element of an amorphous multitude.

On the political level this development led to the formation of mass movements that forced the individual to give up his rights entirely under authoritarian forms of government. Germany was even more prone to dictatorial rule than other countries because extensive industrialization had come very late. The change from a predominantly agrarian to a manufacturing economy did not take place until the realm had finally become politically united as a result of the defeat of the French archenemy in the Franco-Prussian war of 1870–71. The huge reparations payments that France was forced to make provided the financial basis for the industrialization, which spread very rapidly during the final quarter of the nineteenth century and drastically changed the nature of the country and the people. The speed and thoroughness of this fundamental change in the country's economic structure did not give the Germans enough time to adjust, and as a result the loss of traditional values and standards had a very unsettling effect on society. The shock of losing the first World War—because of treachery as many chose to believe—and the militaristic and nationalistic convulsions that followed in the wake of the defeat were signs of the country's social disintegration.

Under these circumstances the Weimar Republic, established in 1919 as the first genuine attempt to introduce democracy to Germany, was built on the shakiest of foundations. Its position was made even more precarious by the rather shortsighted policies of the Allies toward their defeated enemy. The peace treaty of Versailles that had been imposed on the Germans contained many unrealistic conditions designed to prevent them from ever again becoming powerful enough to launch another war. But these same stipulations also in effect denied them the chance to reconstruct their country and restore their national self-respect and sense of dignity. This caused very deep and widespread resentment among the population. People tended to blame the Weimar Republic, whose officials under pressure of an Allied ultimatum had signed the treaty, for the problems created by the terms of the peace agreement. For this reason broad segments of the population regarded the government with a distrustful attitude that burdened still further the newly created democratic institutions.

Matters were made even worse by the fact that the Weimar Republic managed to alienate and disappoint many people on both sides of the political spectrum. The rather idealistic notions of good faith and fair play on which the new state was based and the tendency of the Social Democrats in power to be extremely cautious and often downright calculating made for policies that smacked of compromise and opportunism. Therefore, while from a right-wing perspective the official attitude was still unpalatably radical, on the left many thought their hopes and ideals had been betrayed by the democratic government.

In literary circles this disenchantment with the Weimar Republic was particularly pronounced, and from the middle of the twenties onward there was indeed great and growing cause for concern. More and more the left-wing press was harassed and persecuted with the aid of legal manipulations, including the use of antipornography laws. As early as 1924 the situation had become so serious that the famous journalist Kurt Tucholsky decided to get away from it. He left Berlin and moved to Paris, from where he continued to contribute his satires and penetrating political columns to a number of German publications without having to fear the wrath of the authorities. In the years 1926 and 1927 he also edited from France the highly respected and influential weekly journal *Die Weltbühne.*

If during this period Tucholsky thought that conditions in Germany were bad enough to uproot his private existence and settle in another country, he had seen nothing yet. The Weimar Republic at this time was actually in the midst of a period of relative stability and prosperity. The astute statesmanship of foreign affairs minister Gustav Stresemann had resulted in a reduction of the crippling reparations payments, and the first steps had been taken toward a normalization of Germany's international position. The salutary effects of these achievements could nowhere be seen more clearly than in the complete failure of Hitler's attempted coup in 1923. In December of the following year and again in May 1928 the National Socialists lost heavily

in the Reichstag elections, further indicating that the democracy was in reasonably good shape. If under these auspicious circumstances the Weimar Republic found it necessary to interfere
with the functioning of the free press, it was inevitable that much
harsher repressive measures would be taken when the political
situation took a turn for the worse. In 1929 two events took place
that undid everything that had been gained during the few years
of stabilization and consolidation.

Stresemann, the most successful politician the country had
known at least since World War I, died in October 1929 as in
America the stock market crash ushered in the Great Depression.
Without the man who had been the guiding spirit behind its
efforts to get back on its feet economically and politically, Germany was unable to cope with the greatest crisis the capitalist
world had ever known. Weakened and vulnerable as it still was,
the country suffered more from the international collapse of business and finance than any other nation. As international markets
disappeared and the short-term credits on which the economy
depended dried up, the rug was pulled out from under Germany's
newly achieved relative prosperity. Industry had become overly
concentrated and rationalistic and could not adapt to the crisis.
Unemployment reached catastrophic proportions, and most people, especially on the lower social levels, lived in misery and despair. The resulting chaos and the despondency of the people
provided a fertile soil for extremist ideas and demagogic promises
of revenge. In the elections of 1930 the Nazis increased the
number of seats they held in the Reichstag from 12 to 107. During the following two and a half years the continuing deterioration of the democracy was mirrored in further fascist gains at the
polls. Eventually the National Socialists doubled their 1930 representation in the legislature, making them by far the largest
party in the country.

As such, the fascists successfully persuaded the authorities
by political means and propaganda to step up their pressure on
the liberal and left-radical press. They found that the government
lent a willing ear to these suggestions because under the impact
of the economic crisis a distinctly authoritarian spirit had taken
hold of the republic. At first the parliamentary system was by-

passed through a system of government by decree, and later the legislature was formally dissolved. The growing disregard for democratic procedures was bitterly opposed by the liberal press as far as it could and dared, but all protests were in vain. Tucholsky noted the inability of the printed word to defend the democracy against its enemies and acknowledged the futility of journalistic attempts to turn the political tide. Consequently in 1929 he sharply limited his activity as a publicist and moved from Paris to Sweden, where he lived in the countryside in almost total seclusion. His pessimistic view that public life in Germany had sunk into lawless chaos was confirmed by personal experience. When in November 1929 Tucholsky traveled to Germany to give a lecture in the city of Wiesbaden, fist fights broke out among the audience and a hostile crowd threw stones at his car. In January 1931 Tucholsky told some of his friends that he planned to give up political journalism altogether because it did not pay. He was "fed up" with the hopeless struggle against the forces that were destroying the republic and resigned himself to the inevitable. His skepticism was vindicated when some months later one of his last contributions to the journal *Die Weltbühne* appeared in print. In it he expressed the opinion that soldiers are paid murderers. The officials of the Weimar Republic promptly took legal action against the publication for insulting the armed forces.

Actually the authorities could have spared themselves the trouble because the antifascist press had totally failed to arouse any broad, popular opposition to the ever increasing totalitarian trends. This ineffectiveness was at least partly due to the fact that the progressive intellectuals had become almost completely isolated in their defense of democracy. On the whole even the middle class, to which from a sociological viewpoint they belonged, was either politically indifferent or sympathetic to the cause of the right-wing radicals. At the same time the educated middle-class journalists had little or no success in winning over the proletariat to their liberal views either. The well-meaning appeals to a common interest in the preservation of parliamentary institutions foundered on the workers' traditional distrust of the educated classes, on communication difficulties, and on a fundamental difference in perspective.

The antitotalitarian intellectuals further reduced their own effectiveness by trying, with few exceptions, to influence the course of events from a strictly private standpoint. They based their arguments purely on their own moral authority instead of working through the established structures of political life. Heinrich Mann, for instance, was approvingly dubbed a "politician without a mandate." They may very well have had good reason to shun the parties with their inevitable corruption and compromises. Still, their aloofness certainly robbed them of the only realistic chance of presenting their own views to the general public in an effective manner.[1]

The political impotence of the intellectual middle-class opposition to the National Socialists was made very clear by the lack of any serious resistance to their actual takeover. When early in 1933 the Nazis moved in for the kill, some fitful attempts were made to prevent the worst from happening. But the Germans and their rulers had neither the will and determination nor the strength to withstand Hitler's ruthless singleness of purpose. On 30 January 1933, he became chancellor, and one month later the constitution of the republic was revoked. In the following weeks every vestige of parliamentary government was abolished. In a very short time the fascists established and cemented their absolute dictatorial power over all phases of public and private life in Germany.

The new rulers preached and practiced—as far as others were concerned—the doctrine that the interests of the state came before all individual concerns. Even more important than these collectivist tendencies or their hysterical, aggressive nationalism were their racist dogmas. The main ideological foundation of the Nazi movement and probably the only thing to which Hitler was really committed apart from the pursuit of power was a virulent anti-Semitism. In this connection the fascists could exploit deep-seated sentiments among the German people. Age-old religious hostility against the Jews had since the last part of the nineteenth century been transposed to political, civic, and biological levels. The shifting value standards and life patterns that accompanied Germany's sudden industrialization had caused a breakdown of the traditional social order.

The lower middle classes in particular found it more and more difficult to maintain their status and identity against the politically much more conscious and organized factory proletariat. On other levels the new fluidity of societal standards also led to a sense of insecurity. Unscrupulous propagandists played on these feelings by offering racist discrimination against the Jews as the only firm, reliable standard at a time when all other values seemed to be faltering. Here was a group that everyone could feel superior to, regardless of what happened to their own economic or social standing. From this position it was only a step to blame the Jews for everything that went wrong.

Raised to the level of political principle by the Nazis, anti-Semitism also played a major role in their policies with regard to literature. This was all the more inevitable as Jews did indeed dominate the so-called decadent big city "asphalt literature" that the fascists detested most of all. If a prominent representative of this kind of writing, such as Bertolt Brecht for instance, turned out to be actually "Aryan," the National Socialists simply corrected such awkward facts in their propaganda attacks. They also ignored the many different ideological currents among the progressive writers, who beside socialists and Marxists included anarchists, nihilists, logocrats, and activists of every imaginable stripe. Some of these authors in fact subscribed to distinctly anti-democratic views. It was therefore not surprising that for the less scrupulous among them the fascist movement was not without its redeeming features. Among those in this category who were not barred from doing so by the anti-Semitic rules, some actually joined the Nazi cause.

One of the most notable cases was that of the avant-garde poet Gottfried Benn who with great viciousness turned on his former fellow writers. Others to whom the extremes of the left and right were apparently easily interchangeable included a onetime member of Bertolt Brecht's entourage, Arnold Bronnen, and Ernst von Salomon, who in 1922 had been involved in the murder of foreign affairs minister Walther Rathenau. But these were isolated cases. Almost all progressive and radical writers in Germany remained steadfast in their uncompromising opposition to the National Socialist regime, which meant that the left wing of the

Weimar Republic's literary establishment almost to a man went into exile when Hitler came to power.

The resistance to the fascists was much less unanimous among the other literary schools to be found in Germany during the years preceding the Nazi regime. The reasons for this were partly racial, as the Jews were not particularly prominent in the middle-of-the-road and conservative camps. Diametrically opposite the leftist writers in the broad spectrum of literary currents there existed a reactionary group which, although far from homogeneous, was ideologically centered on the glorious past of the fatherland. Whether idyllic or heroic, the literary visions of these authors tended to idealize earlier times. They were particularly fascinated by the Middle Ages when empire and society offered the security of immutable order. The subjects and ideas that they dealt with in their books were usually quite compatible with the tenor of the Nazi propaganda slogans. For most of the writers who belonged to this school there was consequently neither cause nor necessity to leave the country when the "new order" was established in 1933.

Although quite a few members of this conservative group made common cause with the new rulers, many others did not. Among those who retained their integrity was the well-known novelist Ricarda Huch. Being nearly seventy years old when the Nazis came into power, she stayed in Germany throughout the Third Reich, but she never had anything to do with the fascists either privately or as a writer. Another author who really belonged in the conservative category, although the nature and quality of his work set him apart from the rest, was Stefan George. He too expressed open contempt for the new regime. The snobbish lyric poet headed a circle of like-minded artists in such an autocratic manner that in the literary realm he was no less of a Führer than Hitler in the political sphere. Much of George's verse reads like a sublimation of the Nazi ideology, and some of his formulations were actually adopted by the fascists as political slogans. The poet could have gained official recognition and honor, not to mention material benefit, from this situation, but he refused to sell out. As soon as the National Socialists had taken over the reins of government, he left the country and went to

Switzerland where he died later in the same year. Even in death he left no doubt about his disdain for the Hitler regime. Anticipating that the Nazis would try to claim him for their own after all by giving him an elaborate state funeral, he stipulated in his last will that he was not to be buried in German soil.

In spite of such individual gestures of defiance the conservative literary wing undeniably had a certain ideological affinity with the new regime. A more complex, ambivalent attitude was to be found among those authors who during the twenties and early thirties took up a middle position between radicals and conservatives in the German world of letters. The writers who belonged to this category on the whole came from the upper middle class in which intellectual and artistic interests were traditionally cultivated. These humanists, like the conservatives, were essentially interested in preserving the traditional values, but while they saw the virtues of the past they did not idolize it uncritically. By and large they clung to the humanistic idealism of Germany's great classical authors and philosophers. Nevertheless they recognized that the changing times demanded modifications in this eighteenth-century system of thought to adapt it to the modern era. Politically too they were mindful of tradition but yet within certain limits set by their innate sense of decorum and tradition were willing to accept the need and even the desirability of change and reform.

The rise to power of the fascists confronted these writers with a serious dilemma. On the one hand their origin in well-established bourgeois circles and the widespread illusion that the dictatorship would soon come to an end tended to turn them against the idea of resistance and flight. On the other hand the truly liberal-humanistic outlook of these writers and their pride in a tradition of cultured individualism made the "new order" highly distasteful to them. In some instances inertia and a lack of insight into the true nature of the National Socialist regime tipped the scales in favor of remaining in Germany and coming to terms with the Hitler regime. The elderly dramatist Gerhart Hauptmann, for instance, allowed himself and his reputation to be exploited by the fascists for the purposes of propaganda and representation. For the greater part the more prominent exponents of this group of writers joined the ranks of the exiles. For some of them it was a free choice not to subject themselves and their work to the stifling mental atmosphere of the Third Reich. Often their hand was forced by Germany's new masters who did not tolerate the expression of moderate, truly civilized views.

To some extent at least, the Nazis seem to have been more concerned about the literary opposition they encountered from this liberal-humanistic sector than about the attacks from the radical left wing of the world of letters. On 15 February 1933, for example, the Hitler regime began its direct assault on the literary opposition by throwing Heinrich Mann out of the Prussian Academy of the Arts. One of the foremost representatives of the moderate group, Thomas Mann's older brother had been president of the section for literature of that august institution. The position added prestige to his considerable reputation as a novelist and essayist. Heinrich Mann had used his influence to urge the public in a proclamation drawn up together with the renowned graphic artist Käthe Kollwitz to form a united front of Social Democrats and Communists against the fascists.

This gave the Nazis a welcome excuse to remove him from office and from the Academy altogether. But the real reason Heinrich Mann was the first man of letters to be victimized by the dictatorship went much deeper. Ever since the beginning of the century under the rule of Emperor Wilhelm II, he had been the spokesman for a liberal viewpoint with a pronounced international, specifically French orientation. His outspoken preference for European civilization over German culture was in itself more than enough to make him suspect in the eyes of the Nazis. Heinrich Mann had moreover been one of the few writers of name and reputation who actively supported and endorsed the Weimar Republic. He therefore stood in the way of the National Socialists' efforts to wipe out all traces of the old democratic order and to make the institutions of literary life serve their own demagogic purposes.

Understandably the summary action against Heinrich Mann caused a good deal of consternation and apprehension among writers and other intellectuals. But it was only the beginning.

Less than two weeks later an ominous event on a different scale occurred. In the night of Monday 27 February, the large ornate building in which the Reichstag used to meet was extensively damaged by fire. The Nazis blamed the Communists and used the incident as a pretext for unleashing an obviously well prepared campaign of persecution and terror against all antifascists.

2
Between Two Fires

Even as the black smoke from the gutted Reichstag building still hung in the bleak winter sky over Berlin, the Nazis struck. Some five thousand persons with alleged left-wing sympathies were rounded up and arrested, among them a large number of literary figures and journalists. One of these was Carl von Ossietzky, who had succeeded Kurt Tucholsky as editor of *Die Weltbühne* in 1927. Only a few months earlier Ossietzky had been released from prison after serving a lengthy sentence for publishing an article that exposed the secret and illegal rearmament policy of the Weimar Republic. He had not yet fully recovered from that ordeal when on the morning after the Reichstag fire he was picked up again. This time he was to be held in a concentration camp for five years, during which time the Secret State Police (Gestapo) subjected him to constant physical and mental torture. In 1938 his strength was exhausted and his tormentors released him to die.

Ossietzky had a chance to escape arrest and leave the country in both 1931 and 1933, but since he was an ardent pacifist with an almost excessive sense of moral responsibility, he chose to sacrifice himself to his convictions. Tucholsky from his skeptical viewpoint therefore characterized Ossietzky's fate as a senseless martyrdom. Nevertheless his suffering did serve to reveal the true nature of Hitler's dictatorship to many people who up to that time had not been aware of its potential for evil. His role in awakening world opinion to the reign of terror that had been established in

Germany was recognized with the award of the Nobel Peace Prize in 1935.

The embarrassment that Ossietzky caused the Nazi authorities by staying in Germany from their viewpoint justified the determined effort to drive all antifascist writers and publicists out of the country through intimidation, harassment, and persecution. Goebbels's policy in this regard was from the very beginning quite clear. He assumed that the exiles would lose whatever political influence and strength they might have had and would soon be effectively eliminated as a force to be reckoned with. And the propaganda minister was not alone in thinking that the emigrant authors would be reduced to—as he called them—"cadavers on leave." In a letter written only a week after the Reichstag fire Tucholsky voiced the same opinion. He predicted that the exile literature which would result from the wholesale flight of writers from Germany was doomed to ineffectiveness. Tucholsky foresaw quite accurately that in spite of their good intentions the emigrants would become slightly pathetic, futile figures, endlessly bickering among themselves.

While Tucholsky had no illusions about either the fascists or the exiles, hardly any of those who were being forced to flee the country seemed to have any clear idea of what was in store for them. Although the handwriting had been on the wall for some time, they tended to underestimate the scope of the Nazis' campaign against them. Some, for instance, at first did not actually go abroad when things in Berlin became too dangerous for them but simply moved to Munich. They assumed that because of Germany's peculiar political structure, which allowed much autonomy to the individual states, Bavaria would somehow escape the Nazi stranglehold. As a matter of fact the local government there did at first proclaim its determination to defend its independence from Prussia, but rhetoric could hardly stem the political tide. Two weeks after the Reichstag fire Hitler successfully "parallelized" Bavaria—as the total subjugation under Berlin was called—and the Munich populace enthusiastically hailed the new Nazi governor.

Those who had sought refuge in Munich now had to move on and were joined in their continued flight by many of the local literati. The most famous of these, Thomas Mann, at the time happened to be out of the country. He was vacationing in Switzerland after a lecture tour that had taken him to several western European countries, and after the "parallelization" decided to stay abroad indefinitely. The fine distinction that he had not actually left the country to go into exile but had simply not returned to it would later be used by some to argue that he did not really belong to the literary emigration.

It casts a revealing light on the political naiveté of Thomas Mann that his son Klaus and daughter Erika had considerable difficulty in persuading him to stay abroad. They had seen the effects of the nazification of Munich and had become aware that the fascists were planning to take action against their father, or at least put pressure on him to change his critical attitude toward the new rulers. Hints by the family driver, who later turned out to have been a Nazi agent but apparently still had some feelings of loyalty toward his employer, further convinced Klaus and Erika that they should warn Thomas Mann not to come home.

Knowing that the telephone was most likely tapped, they tried to get the message across to their father by harping on the weather, which they insisted was much too bad for him to return. He did not understand their allusions at all and insisted somewhat testily that he was coming back to Munich as planned. Finally his children had to take the risk of telling him openly that the political conditions made it necessary for him to stay in Switzerland. Mann's unsuspecting attitude and his determination to go home in spite of the nazification of Munich are all the more surprising since his lecture tour had been viciously criticized in Germany. A group of prominent Nazi artists including the composer Richard Strauss and the conductor Hans Knappertsbusch had claimed that his featured talk about Richard Wagner was an insult to the German genius.

Meanwhile the fascists proceeded apace with their efforts to regulate literary life in Germany in keeping with their own ideas and aims. In doing so they concentrated on the section for literature of the Prussian Academy for the Arts. The twenty-seven members who remained after the purge of 15 February were asked in the middle of March to sign a declaration of loyalty to the new regime drawn up by Gottfried Benn. Eighteen of them complied, and six either did not react at all or gave an ambiguous reply. Thomas Mann, novelist Alfred Döblin, who by this time was also already abroad, and Ricarda Huch took the opportunity to withdraw voluntarily as a gesture of protest against the developments since Heinrich Mann's ouster as president. Early in May those who had not signed the declaration were formally removed from the Academy. The same thing happened to several of the members who had declared their loyalty to the fascists but who were held to be racially, ideologically, or artistically undesirable.

The seats on the Academy that had become vacant in this way were filled with writers who could be counted upon to serve the interests of the National Socialists. They were on the whole men of inferior artistic stature and lesser reputation than the writers they replaced. The tone was set by Heinrich Mann's successor as president of the section for literature, the obscure novelist Hans Friedrich Blunck, who was appointed after Stefan George had refused the honor. Blunck's preference for regional themes from his north German homeland and his preoccupation with the history and legends of the Teutonic peoples were entirely consistent with the Nazis' ideological stress on "blood and soil."

Blunck's literary caliber and that of most other new members gave substance to the exiles' view that the Academy had been turned into a "barbers' club" and a "poetasters' circle." The generally low quality of their protégés forced the Nazis for reasons of prestige and propaganda to try to win over to their side some prominent figures. They made sizable ideological concessions to those they wanted to enlist into their ranks. Ricarda Huch's open act of defiance in resigning from the Academy, for instance, was ignored and neither she personally nor her books were boycotted. But the proud old lady refused to be taken in.

The door was also left ajar with the same lack of success in the case of Thomas Mann. His studied aloofness with respect to the rank and file exiles raised Nazi hopes that he might be willing to come to terms with them. As a world famous novelist and Nobel Prize winner he would have been an extremely valuable ally for the new regime. It was at the same time a warning and a hint of their willingness to let bygones be bygones if Mann chose to cooperate that the Nazis included only one early, minor publication of his among a number of authors and works blacklisted at the end of April.

This list prepared the way for the climax of the Nazi campaign against their literary enemies, which in its brutality has become a symbol of totalitarian terrorism. On 10 May 1933, the wave of persecution and intimidation that had begun with the Reichstag fire culminated in another conflagration as hundreds of thousands of books were publicly burned throughout Germany. Mass ceremonies at which those works the fascists deemed to be particularly hostile or detrimental to their cause were committed to the flames took place in all university towns. Especially in Berlin the occasion was turned into a large and elaborate demonstration against the intellectuals and men of letters that Germany's new masters sought to silence and destroy. According to a report of the event that appeared in the *Neuköllner Tageblatt* of 12 May 1933, before the actual book burning began the newly appointed professor of political pedagogy Alfred Bäumler delivered his inaugural lecture. The university auditorium was filled to overflowing, mainly with students wearing the uniform of the SA, the Nazi paramilitary terror organization. After a group of them had marched in with the swastika flag, the professor took the floor to hold forth on the intellectual and philosophical aspects of the National Socialist movement. He told his audience that in the political sense the revolution was all but completed but that spiritually and socially it had only just begun. According to Bäumler, youth and particularly students had a vital role to play in the implementation of the fascist ideals. These allusions to the planned book burning were not lost on his audience, which responded with great gusto to the professorial words.

When the lecture was over the students gathered outside the university and accompanied by a brass band marched to a nearby fraternity house. When they arrived there at half-past nine they were given torches and detailed instructions. A large crowd was on hand to watch these preparations, which were concluded with another speech. One of the officials of the National Socialist student organization called for an attack on the un-German spirit and on bad books. The assembled students were told to wipe out everything unwholesome from the hearts and minds of their fellow citizens.

After this talk the students, led by Professor Bäumler, marched through the streets of Berlin with their musical accompaniment and carts full of "decadent" books to be burned. Around eleven o'clock they arrived at the partly cordoned off Opera Square and threw their torches onto the pyre that had been erected in the center. As the flames leapt up students formed a human chain to pass the books from hand to hand, and soon the first of more than twenty thousand volumes were consumed by the fire. The crowd cheered wildly and then listened to a brief speech by one of the student leaders.

Then while brass bands of the SA and SS played rousing march music, nine representatives of the student body took turns throwing books into the flames. They had been assigned specific subject areas and authors, and as they added their share to the bonfire they cried:

"Against class struggle and materialism, for solidarity of the people and an idealistic outlook on life! I surrender to the flames the writings of Marx and Kautsky."

"Against decadence and moral decay! For discipline and decency in family and state! I surrender to the flames the writings of Heinrich Mann, Ernst Glaeser, and Erich Kästner."

"Against manipulation of opinion and political treachery, for devotion to people and state! I surrender to the flames the writings of Friedrich Wilhelm Förster."

"Against the overevaluation of instinctual urges that destroy the soul, for the nobility of the soul! I surrender to the flames the writings of Sigmund Freud."

"Against falsification of our history and degradation of its great figures, for respect for our past! I surrender to the flames the writings of Emil Ludwig and Werner Hegemann."

"Against the democratic-Jewish kind of journalism that is alien to the people, for responsible collaboration on the work of national construction! I surrender to the flames the writings of Theodor Wolff and Georg Bernhard."

"Against literary betrayal of the soldiers of the World War, for the education of the people in the spirit of truthfulness! I surrender to the flames the writings of Erich Maria Remarque."

"Against arrogant botching of the German language, for the preservation of the people's valuable possession! I surrender to the flames the writings of Alfred Kerr."

"Against impudence and insolence, for esteem and reverence for the immortal spirit of the German people! Devour, flames, also the writings of Tucholsky and Ossietzky!"

Some of those whose books were burned for the sake of the Nazi-style purification of the German spirit had by this time been imprisoned or placed in detention camps. Others had already left the country. But those who had so far hesitated to go into exile at this point almost to a man fled the country. Other writers who had not been included in the book burning but who knew that the shoe fit them as well were also prompted to leave Germany by this demonstration of barbarity. And so within a period of some three months after coming to power, the National Socialists had succeeded in driving practically the entire literary opposition into exile. This included almost all writers of any consequence. It has been estimated that by the end of May 1933 close to fifteen hundred reputable professional men of letters had turned their backs on the Third Reich.

But in leaving Germany they had by no means given up their opposition to the fascist regime. On the contrary, their flight was to a large extent motivated by the determination to continue the struggle, which under the circumstances was possible only from beyond the borders. The Nazi book burnings themselves became the object of defiant gestures by some authors such as the novelist Hermynia zur Mühlen who publicly protested that her works had not also been cast into the flames. A similar attitude was taken by Oskar Maria Graf whose books were not only spared from burning but even recommended to the German reading public by the Nazis.

One of the first to leave the country, Graf had always belonged to the political left and had never made any attempt to hide his Marxist leanings. A few days before the book burnings he had publicly announced his resignation from the Bavarian branch of the official writers' organization. On that occasion he had explicitly declared his solidarity with those writers who were being persecuted and forced into exile. In many other cases this kind of attitude was enough to insure the writer concerned a place on every list of undesirable elements and enemies of the Third Reich, but Graf's political sympathies were studiously over-looked by the fascists. Furthermore only one of his books, the autobiographical novel *Prisoners All* (*Wir sind Gefangene*) was banned. Apparently the censors disapproved of the description of Graf's successful attempt to evade the military draft in World War I by getting himself declared insane and unfit for active service.

All of Graf's other works continued to be sold in Germany, and the Nazis had their reasons for this permissiveness. It is not hard to see why Graf, in spite of his communism and antipatriot-ic attitude, did not share the fate of practically all his likeminded colleagues whose work was promptly banned in its entirety. For one thing Graf was of pure Germanic stock without any trace of Jewish or other foreign elements. Moreover he wrote novels based on his own background as the child of a Bavarian farm laborer— exactly the kind of thing the Nazis needed to support their "blood and soil" doctrine. And while there were many other novelists of the rustic life, none of them was either as talented and reputable or as experienced and well informed as Oskar Maria Graf.

That Graf's publications were not burned and with one excep-tion were even included on the "white list" of officially approved and recommended reading matter was intended as an inducement to reap the rewards of collaboration with Germany's new masters. But the novelist spurned the attempt to bribe him into playing along with the fascists. On 11 May, the day after the book burn-ing, he wrote an open letter to the National Socialist authorities under the headline "Burn me!" Published in the *Wiener Arbeiter-zeitung* and other papers, it noted that he had apparently been chosen as one of the representatives of the new German spirit and continued:

I ask myself in vain why I have deserved this humiliation. The Third Reich has expelled almost all of its important writers, has divorced itself from the real German literature, has chased the great majority of its significant authors into exile and prohibited the publication of their works in Germany. The ignorance of a few pretentious literary opportunists and the unbridled vandalism of the currently ruling authorities try to exterminate all those aspects of our literature and art which enjoy world recognition, and to replace the concept "German" with narrow minded nationalism. A nationalism on whose command my forthright socialist comrades are persecuted, incarcerated, tortured, murdered or driven to suicide out of despair! And the representatives of this barbaric nationalism which has nothing, absolutely nothing to do with German-ness have the impudence to claim me as one of their "spiritual allies," to put me on their so-called white list, which in the conscience of the world can only be a black list.

This dishonor I have not deserved!

After the life I have lived and the books I have written I have a right to demand that my books are surrendered to the pure flame of the pyre and do not get into the bloody hands and the depraved brains of the fascist murderers!

Burn the works of the German spirit! It will be inextinguishable, like your shame!

Even after this provocative open letter had been printed, the regime did not immediately give up all ideas of using Graf's talent for their own purposes. As late as the end of 1933 the novelist complained bitterly in another open letter to the authorities that two of his books were still not listed on the index of banned works. Although the Nazis at first had been rather haphazard in compiling their various lists of names and titles that were taboo, by this time such omissions could no longer be attributed to mere oversight. An elaborate bureaucracy had been brought into being to codify and enforce the various measures aimed at wiping out all opposition literature. No fewer than seventeen offices and organizations had been created by the government to supervise all aspects of literary life, including the activities of authors, publishers, printers, and book dealers. As early as 16 May 1933 an official black list of 131 exiled authors and their works had been published.

The authorities operated on guidelines that defined four categories of writers whose books were to be banned. All "non-Aryans," including mainly the Jews but also members of other "inferior races" such as Gypsies, constituted one group. Another bracket consisted of members of the Communist Party and others who were considered to have Marxist sympathies. Also banned were the writings of anyone who had ever published anything critical of National Socialism. In November 1933 the Nazis formed a national literary organization called the "Reichsschrifttumskammer" in order to have more direct and unified control over the remaining journalists and authors. Anyone who refused to join this body was automatically outlawed. Beginning on 23 August the fascists also periodically published lists of writers who had gone into exile and thereby forfeited their German citizenship. Whatever property and possessions they left behind in Germany were confiscated by the state and their entire literary work was banned, including any titles that up to that time had not been censored.

By their organized and relentless suppression of the literary opposition, the fascists naturally provoked the emigrant authors to ever more implacable hatred toward their regime. So the events brought to a climax by the book burnings crystallized the antagonism between the Nazis and the large and vehemently antifascist literary exile. The irreconcilable ideological differences that separated the two sides were very clearly reflected in a verbal duel between Thomas Mann's son Klaus, already a well-known writer in his own right, and Gottfried Benn.

In the years around World War I when the expressionist movement was at its height, Benn had made a name for himself with his particularly cynical and nihilistic brand of lyric poetry. In the Weimar Republic he enjoyed a certain fame and reputation in the more progressive literary circles for his experimental prose. The radical essays he wrote during this time were marked by anti-intellectual tendencies that betrayed an affinity with Nazi ideology. Even so it came as a shock to many of his former friends and associates that Benn enthusiastically welcomed Hitler's dictatorship as the realization of his own ideals. On 24 April he held an infamous radio talk on "The New State and the Intellectuals." He derided all liberalism and proclaimed that intellectual freedom had to be subordinated and sacrificed to the totalitarian state. At the same time he hailed the National Socialists as representing the new heroic biological type to which the future belonged.

Speaking for those who were angry and upset about Benn's unscrupulous stab in the back, Klaus Mann on 9 May wrote him an open letter. Mann identified himself with the many admirers that Benn once had among the younger generation, who were now dismayed by their idol's fall. He respectfully raised the question how someone whose name had been synonymous with the highest moral level and with an almost fanatical purity of spirit could in this critical hour lend his support to the Nazis. The letter went on to point out that Benn had been the only one among the authors on whom the antifascists had counted who had let them down. He had not resigned from the Academy of the Arts and had made common cause with people whom Mann called unsavory and contemptible. These new associates were then contrasted with the exiles who both personally and artistically belonged to a superior type and who would still welcome Benn to their ranks. Klaus Mann further postulated that Benn's attitude was really rooted in his dislike of certain Marxist writers and their practices. But although this antipathy was justifiable enough in itself, Benn had, according to the open letter, allowed himself to overreact. The fascist politics that he had embraced went to even greater extremes of irrationalism than the Communism he rejected. Perhaps more to the point was Klaus Mann's observation that the repudiation of civilization which forms a constant theme in Benn's work was dangerously close to the worship of brute power.

Gottfried Benn answered Klaus Mann's letter in a radio talk on 24 May which on the following day was also published in the press. This "Answer to the Literary Emigrants" took Mann's remarks only as the occasion for a general attack on the exiles. Benn accused them of cowardice in not having stayed in Germany to experience the rise of the new state at first hand and denied them the right to criticize the Nazi regime from the outside. In the most turgid images and expressions Benn defended his own fascist ideology against the rational and progressive outlook of the new regime's opponents. He claimed that his own views were based on primeval creative forces.

In his answer to the exiles Benn made little or no attempt to come to grips with the issues raised by Klaus Mann. The radio address was really aimed over the heads of the emigrants at the German listening public and was carefully calculated to arouse strong feelings against the exiles. Benn had chosen his words so as to discredit as much as possible those who had left their country in order to remain free to raise their voice against Hitler. But Benn's attempt to ingratiate himself with the guardians of the "new order" misfired. Klaus Mann had concluded his letter with the prediction that Benn's alliance with the Nazis would yield him nothing but contempt and scorn from their side also. It soon became apparent that the fascists did indeed have no use whatsoever for the poet who from their viewpoint exemplified the worst kind of artistic decadence. In October 1933 Benn in another radio talk on "Breeding and Future" again tried to establish himself as a bona fide fascist by praising the Nazi ideal of Germanic racial purity, but the authorities were not impressed. They had in fact by this time decided to disown him completely and for that reason branded the would-be apostle of "Aryanism" himself as a Jew.

As a result of this Benn not only lost his license to practice medicine but was also violently attacked for the alleged criminal indecency and immorality of his writings. He tried to defend himself by protesting that he was a purebred German untainted by any Jewish blood—which was true—and by showing his loyalty to the regime in further public utterances. But he soon realized that these efforts to win the favor of the Nazis were in vain, and by the end of 1934 the error of his ways had become fully clear to him. He tried to reestablish contact with those of his former friends who although antifascist were still in Germany. Understandably his advances were met with great caution and skepticism. Benn then sought refuge in the relatively neutral political atmosphere of the army, where his medical expertise in venereal disease was put to good use.

3
The Cassandra Syndrome

Even though the exiles saw the true nature of the Hitler dictatorship much more clearly than Gottfried Benn, they grossly misjudged the staying power of the new German regime. Most of the writers who had been forced to leave the country during the first months of 1933 assumed that their banishment would not last long. They could simply not imagine that a government which had so blatantly demonstrated its utter contempt for the basic principles of justice and political morality would be able to stay in power for any length of time. The exiles persuaded themselves and assured each other that it was a matter of a few weeks or at most some months before the German people would come to their senses and put an end to the fascist reign of terror. Most emigrants therefore embarked on their odyssey much as if it were a kind of involuntary holiday. Klaus Mann was a typical case in this respect. He packed only one or two suitcases and took nothing with him except two suits, some underwear, a few books, and his manuscripts.

As the Nazis in the months following their rise to power settled in with the apparent support of the general population, the emigrants were forced to face the fact that they would not be going home any time soon. They had all the more cause to regret their initial optimism as the German authorities confiscated any property they had left behind. In addition the Nazis demanded where applicable payment of a special tax for leaving the country, which had been instituted by the Weimar Republic in 1931. It amounted to 25 percent of the emigrant's capital over 200,000 marks and of his annual income over 20,000 marks. The tax was not levied if the person concerned continued to pay his regular taxes in Germany for a period of five years after he went abroad.

Until May 1934 the National Socialists applied this taxation as they had inherited it from their predecessors. Then the exemption clause for those who contributed normal revenue for five years was eliminated and the capital deduction was reduced to 50,000 marks. Even so, only a few writers were affluent enough to fall under the provisions of this law, and those who did were understandably enough reluctant to pay up, although refusal to do so could weaken the legal status of those who still had financial or other interests in Germany.

On the whole the most serious measure taken against the exiles by the German government was the revocation of their citizenship status. The exiles had at first been inclined to underrate the effect of this move, on the assumption that foreign officials would be certain to sympathize with their plight and their cause and make allowances for their special circumstances. But as it soon turned out, the lack of valid travel documents and identity papers made it very difficult for the stateless authors to live, travel, and work abroad. They had been wrong in counting on the sympathetic understanding of foreign governments. The countries in which they sought refuge continued to insist in varying degrees on all the formalities connected with entry, residence, and labor permits. The attempts to get these papers led to many humiliating and frustrating confrontations with the foreign bureaucrats who went strictly by the letter of the law. Many exiles found these clashes with officialdom among the most traumatic aspects of the entire exile experience.

Language barriers inevitably compounded the difficulties that faced the emigrants in their efforts to settle in a host country. This was undoubtedly one of the main reasons why in the early years of the Nazi regime many of those who had to leave Germany went to Austria. Hitler's homeland was the largest German-speaking area not yet under Nazi control. Because of their familiarity with the language and ways of life there, the emigrants found it much easier to cope with the system in Austria than in any other country. Austria also offered the best personal and professional amenities to the antifascist writers. There were many German language publishing houses, newspapers and journals, and no legislation to hinder or prevent the emigrants from taking part in literary life. The relatively good opportunities to appear in print enabled quite a few of the exiles to earn a living, although not usually on the same level as they had enjoyed in Germany. Equally important was the fact that in Austria they could write for a public that was conditioned by much the same cultural and literary traditions as their German readers from whom they were now almost completely cut off. In any case Vienna scarcely counted as foreign territory to most German writers, many of whom had previously lived and worked there at some time. A number of the authors expelled by the fascists actually were Austrians who had earlier moved to Germany.

Yet in spite of its considerable advantages, very few of the exiles made an effort to settle permanently in Austria because of the political situation there. The government represented a peculiarly Austrian brand of clerical fascism. It distinguished itself favorably from the German variety by the absence of anti-Semitic doctrines. Nevertheless it was totalitarian in nature and pursued a harshly repressive policy toward the left-wing parties. The internal tensions and instability of the country together with political developments in Europe generally boded ill for the future. Viennese journalist Karl Kraus remarked of the arriving exiles: "The rats are boarding the sinking ship." Under these circumstances most of them preferred to move on to other places of refuge.

Czechoslovakia attracted many emigrants by its liberal political climate and its geographic location, for it was easy to reach from both Germany and Austria. Another point in its favor was the existence of an old established German-speaking middle-class community in the capital city of Prague, which formed at least a basis for literary and journalistic enterprise. The significance of this cultural enclave can be gauged from the fact that such talented writers as Franz Kafka and Franz Werfel arose from it, to mention only two of the best-known "Prague-German" authors. This linguistic minority group traditionally supported a certain amount of publishing activity, but the production of newspapers, journals, and books was by no means large enough to absorb the contributions of the exiles.

The new arrivals therefore founded a number of publications and presses to serve their own needs. Through these specifically exile oriented media they could give much clearer voice to their particular concerns than in Austria where they had to express themselves within the framework of the established organs. In its diversity the emigrant press reflected the wide political range of the exile community in Czechoslovakia. It included many different positions, which centered on such organizations as a writers' chapter of the "League for Human Rights," a literary section of the Marxist "Bertolt Brecht Club," and the humanistic "Thomas Mann Club." But even though the spectrum of ideological groupings reached all the way from right to left, the Communists had a large majority in the Czechoslovak exile community.

In the major emigrant journals based in Prague, for instance, Thomas Mann was consistently attacked. Especially the first volume of his four-part novel *Joseph and his Brothers* (*Joseph und seine Brüder*) which appeared in 1933 was sharply criticized. The *Neue Deutsche Blätter* objected to the novel and its biblical subject matter, calling it escapist because it did not deal directly with current political realities. This insistence on literature that was explicitly antifascist was rooted in the editors' dogmatic commitment to the cause of radical socialism.

The political bias of the refugee community in Prague was also much in evidence in the machinations surrounding another exile journal published there, *Die Neue Weltbühne*. It was the direct successor of the publication edited by Tucholsky and Ossietzky, which even in the closing years of the Weimar Republic had been in danger of being banned. At that time an imminent Nazi takeover already seemed more than probable, and with it the certain end of the journal. Plans were therefore laid for a parallel edition to be published in Vienna by renegade Communist newspaperman Willi Schlamm. Under the name *Wiener Weltbühne*, this offshoot commenced publication in the spring of 1932. It consisted mainly of articles taken from the original German journal, supplemented by an editorial from the pen of Schlamm and a few local contributions. Schlamm had the sole responsibility for editorial policy. In business matters he shared authority with the widow of the *Weltbühne*'s founder, Mrs. Jacobsohn, and the Jewish Viennese chocolate manufacturer Heller, who had financed the venture.

After Ossietzky had been arrested by the Nazis and on 7 March 1933 the Berlin *Weltbühne* was permanently banned, the Viennese publication took over, changing its name to *Die Neue Weltbühne*. Although this maneuver saved the journal for the time being, its troubles were by no means over. The political atmosphere in Austria gave ample cause for concern about the future. More specifically Schlamm had endangered his own position in his homeland through his sharp attacks on Chancellor Schuschnigg's "labor-hostile, fascist, murderous" policies. For these reasons in April 1933 the editorial and publishing headquarters of *Die Neue Weltbühne* were moved to Prague. There the editor tried to adapt the journal to the political situation of the day. He transformed it from a platform for nonaligned left-wing intellectuals into an organ for the opposition "against both deadly dangers that confront the west—Nazism and bolshevism."

In the context of this program Schlamm published a series of articles by Stalin's enemy Leon Trotsky. In the eyes of the faithful Communists this was the crowning insult. They hated Schlamm anyway for having earlier defected from the Party and moreover wanted to get hold of the prestigious *Weltbühne* as a propaganda vehicle for their own party line. They therefore spread the tale that Schlamm had somehow improperly grabbed control of the journal and abused it in a Trotskyite spirit. To the doctrinaire Marxist mind this was a serious allegation, but in their efforts to discredit Schlamm the Party stalwarts went much further than that. In Prague alone within the space of a single month more than fifty articles appeared in which he was smeared and denounced. He was accused of all kinds of base misdeeds. Being a secret Gestapo agent was one of the relatively lesser infamies imputed to him.

Schlamm's enemies did not limit themselves to slander and character assassination. They also intrigued to force him out of his editorial position. If he gave up control of the journal, they

could with the aid of Mrs. Jacobsohn turn *Die Neue Weltbühne* into a tool of the Communist Party. Once they had prepared the
way with their public defamation of Schlamm, an elaborate plot
to oust him was set in motion. Mrs. Jacobsohn started bombarding him with letters protesting the alleged anti-Marxist attitude
of the journal. Schlamm objected to this interference on the basis
that his contract guaranteed editorial autonomy. When Mrs.
Jacobsohn reacted to his remonstration with an even more strongly worded letter, he flew to Zurich, where she lived at that time,
and offered his resignation. She accepted it straightway and in the
same breath appointed as his successor a man who as it now
appeared had during their discussion been waiting in an adjoining room. He was Hermann Budzislawski, an entirely loyal Communist Party member. Schlamm now realized that he had fallen
into a trap and that the entire incident had been intentionally
provoked in order to play *Die Neue Weltbühne* into Marxist hands.
He promptly withdrew his resignation.

According to the terms of the contract, conflicts of this nature
between the shareholders concerning noneditorial matters had to
be submitted to an independent arbitrator. The party found to be
in the wrong was then to sell its interests in the journal. From
Zurich Schlamm went to Vienna and there agreed with the other
partner, Heller, to put these provisions into effect. But the course
of political events scuttled his plan. In February 1934, before the
hearing could be scheduled, an uprising of the Social Democrats
took place in the Austrian capital. As a result the attitude of the
regime of Chancellor Dollfuß toward the left-wing parties became
even more hostile than before.

Three days later Heller received a letter from Budzislawski
threatening legal action for defamation of character if the planned
arbitration procedure was not immediately canceled. Such a court
case would in the prevailing tense political atmosphere have had
very serious consequences for Heller. Although not systematically
persecuted by the Dollfuß government, the Jews were far from
popular and in any crisis tended to be made the scapegoat. If his
connection with the *Weltbühne*, which was most unpopular in
ruling circles, had become publicly known in the course of the
lawsuit threatened by Budzislawski, Heller would have been in

serious trouble. He therefore suggested that the case be brought to court in Prague instead of Vienna, but Budzislawski knew that he had the upper hand and rejected the proposal. The Communist's contemptible blackmail tactic paid off because in this situation Schlamm yielded the editorship rather than expose Heller to the wrath of the Austrian authorities. Budzislawski immediately turned *Die Neue Weltbühne* into a Communist Party sheet.

The Marxist refugees had no monopoly on intrigues and other dubious tactics against their rivals within the emigration. A pendant to the *Neue Weltbühne* affair can be found in the equally unsavory machinations involving a journal published in Amsterdam. Holland in this early phase was a center of liberal and humanistically oriented exiles who were usually not closely tied to any specific party line. Although there was no German-speaking intelligentsia such as existed in Prague, conditions were quite favorable for the refugees. The Dutch people on the whole and the literary circles in particular were deeply involved in the events that were taking place in Germany. Their concern over the rise of fascism across the border was partly due to the close economic and linguistic ties between the two countries. The violent anti-Semitism of the Nazis was in any case particularly distasteful and shocking to a people who were traditionally free from racist delusions.

The prevailing mood in Holland made it possible for the antifascist exiles to establish good rapport with the native literary and intellectual circles. The generally sympathetic attitude toward the emigrants bore fruit in the foundation of several publishing ventures. Two of the best known publishers in Amsterdam went so far as to set up German-language sections specifically to handle works by refugees from the Third Reich. As early as 1933 both the publishing firms Allert de Lange and Querido appointed exiled former editors of the German publishing house of Kiepenheuer to direct their activities in this area.

As part of its German program Querido brought out one of the most distinguished journals of the early exile period. *Die Sammlung* appeared from September 1933 until August 1935 under the editorship of Klaus Mann. Its contributors came from every segment of the political spectrum and often within one and the same issue expressed contradictory opinions even on such basic questions as the nature of fascism. This lack of a clear ideological line was in itself indicative of the journal's basic liberal attitude, which reflected Klaus Mann's own views.

Much more than other exile periodicals *Die Sammlung* tried to go beyond the narrow range of interests most vital to the expatriates. As an integral part of its editorial policy the journal opened its pages not only to German antifascists but also to other European and American writers. Both the international orientation of *Die Sammlung* and its broadly humanistic political and ideational position were reflected in the patronage of André Gide, Aldous Huxley, and Heinrich Mann. It published work by many of the prominent exiles and by such notable figures from the international world of letters as Romain Rolland, Jean Cocteau, Benedetto Croce, Ignazio Silone, Stephen Spender, Christopher Isherwood, Ernest Hemingway, Pär Lagerkvist, and Boris Pasternak. As this impressive list indicates, the journal had a pronounced literary character, but this did not imply an attitude of apolitical aestheticism. Literature was regarded as a most vital expression of the spirit of civilization that was endangered by the advent of fascist totalitarianism.

It was this conception of literary relevance in the face of Nazi persecution and terror that touched off one of the most disconcerting incidents in the history of exile writing. It cast a very harsh light if not on the ethics at least on the political judgment of some of the most prominent exiles. Klaus Mann's editorial direction apparently troubled the Nazis considerably, and they tried to contain the danger they saw in *Die Sammlung* by means of intimidation. Shortly after the first issue had come out, the German authorities published a stern warning against any form of collaboration with the exile press and particularly with *Die Sammlung*. It was addressed to those authors who had gone abroad but whose work at this early point could still be sold within Germany. The fascists threatened them with a total ban if they continued to support the emigrant periodical. Such action would have been a blow not only to the authors themselves but even more to the business interests of their publishers. The major book firms therefore pressured the writers in question to disown

Die Sammlung. The authors were promised that these statements would be kept confidential, and quite a number of them fell into the trap. As soon as they complied, their declarations were published by the jubilant Nazis.

Some of these men of letters made a point of explicitly dissociating themselves from the political orientation of the periodical. René Schickele for instance declared that he was "painfully surprised by the political character of *Sammlung* because occasional contribution only to purely literary journal had been proposed." And Schickele contritely promised to mend his ways: "Am in no way connected with Querido, will also in future have nothing to do with things of this sort." Alfred Döblin's telegram read: "Disavow all literary and political association with editor of the journal *Sammlung*. Request that this be made known in appropriate way as soon as possible. Bias of the journal was not known by me." Even Thomas Mann renounced his son's journal in a telegram which stated that he "could only confirm that the character of the first issue of *Die Sammlung* does not conform to its original program." In view of the fact that the journal's only political commitment was to an uncompromising antifascism, the inescapable conclusion is that these writers did not want to offend the Nazis.

Several different explanations for their dubious attitude in the *Sammlung* affair have been given by the authors themselves and by others. Thomas Mann and René Schickele may seriously have believed that the humanistic spirit of their work could effectively stimulate the opposition against fascist totalitarianism within Germany. From that standpoint they would have been right in doing everything possible to make sure that the German reading public could continue to read their books. But if that was the reason for renouncing Klaus Mann and his journal, it implies at the very least a crass overestimation of the power of the literary word and an equally drastic underestimation of the National Socialists. The real result of their decision to give in to the Nazi threats was a propaganda victory for the Hitler regime. The fact that books by reputable nonfascists were for the time being still for sale could be used to refute accusations that all cultural freedom was being stifled in the Third Reich.

Alfred Döblin explained his disavowal of *Die Sammlung* as the result of personal pressures. He had been visited in his French place of exile by a representative of his publisher who urged him to make a statement along these lines. In order to add weight to his suggestion this gentleman, who incidentally was a Jew himself, had hinted that if Döblin did not comply the novelist's two eldest sons who were in Germany at the time would be in danger of being sent to a concentration camp. And indeed as soon as his sons were in safety Döblin contributed to *Die Sammlung*. Yet on the whole the suspicion remains that those who betrayed Klaus Mann on this issue were also conscious of their own financial interests at stake in a ban on the lucrative sale of their works in Nazi Germany. Most of them moreover took a long time before trying to explain or excuse their gross disloyalty to the exile cause.

But there was at least one writer—wealthy enough certainly not to have to worry about the loss of some royalties—whose conscience reacted more quickly. Stefan Zweig also had repudiated *Die Sammlung* at the request of his publisher. Only about a month later in November 1933 he retracted his statement. Zweig pointed to the fundamental fallacy on which his original statement had been based and acknowledged the inescapable fact that the exile had no choice but total severance of all ties with the Nazi state: "It simply is not possible to publish in Germany and write in journals against Germany. But now the decision has been taken— one cannot have anything more to do with Germany, I burn all bridges."

Apart from all personal motives and opinions the criticisms of Klaus Mann's political approach to exile literature touched on a fundamental problem. It was soon to become the central issue in all discussions about the true nature and function of exile writing. The matter was first raised openly by the young Dutch writer Menno ter Braak. As a dedicated antifascist he was deeply involved in the activities of the German exile colony in Amsterdam. In December 1934 he published an essay in vol. 52 of the influential exile journal *Neues Tage Buch* dealing with "Emigrant Literature." Ter Braak expressed his disappointment that the writers who had been driven out of Germany by the Nazis had so far not come forth with any "real emigration literature," which he defined as writing that "differs essentially from the pre-Hitler production." According to the Dutchman, the exile authors carried on business as usual. As far as possible under the prevailing extraordinary circumstances they wrote the same kinds of works as before they had left Germany. Ter Braak claimed they did not come to grips with the radically changed political situation, which according to him made all writing purely for art's sake redundant. As he put it, "Well written, tastefully composed books which could have been written by any other talented author and don't offer the reader anything more than 'other' good books are relatively . . . meaningless. It is something else that matters. The emigration should be more than a continuation. It should have the courage to understand its European task and not let its attitude toward literature be affected only by the necessity to fight against the false mysticism of the 'blood-and-soil' cultists."

Ter Braak not only attacked the lack of political relevance of exile writing but also its literary quality. In his opinion the artistic level suffered from the habit of most emigrant journals to be far too lavish in their praise of new works by refugees. On both counts the Dutchman's views provoked heated rebuttals from some German expatriates, who argued that exaggeratedly positive reviews were often a matter of survival in the very restricted market in which the exile presses operated. The lack of outstanding quality in exile writing was tacitly acknowledged, but an attempt was made to excuse and defend it with the observation that mediocrity was an inevitable part of the literary scene. According to this view the authors had no other duty than to do the best they could. This amounted to a direct contradiction of Ter Braak's views by calling for an exile literature that would basically be a continuation of the writing practiced in pre-Nazi Germany.

Obviously this implied a divergence of talents and objectives among the emigrants rather than a single-minded universal antifascist hard line. From the viewpoint of Ter Braak's critics it would indeed be wrong to expect unity of purpose or achievement from the exiles. It was argued that the emigration included people with widely differing political and artistic ideas who had nothing in common except the fate of being exiled. Ludwig Marcuse was one of those who held that it was impossible to assign specific characteristics or functions to emigrant literature. Early in 1935 he expressed his views on the matter in an article in *Neues Tage Buch*: "The phenomenon that is called 'emigrant literature' is . . . nothing more than the sum of all the books of authors writing in German who since Hitler's coronation either *cannot* appear in Germany anymore or do not *want* to appear in Germany anymore, or neither can nor want to. This social situation which a number of German writers have in common does not however amount to even a minimal literary community. Such a community does not exist on an extra-literary plane either, not even in the sense of kindred political impulses."

The opposing views held by Menno ter Braak and Ludwig Marcuse mark the two schools of thought that determined the directions of anti-Nazi writing until the end of the emigration. The Dutch critic's comments really amounted to a call for texts that subordinated everything else to the direct, explicit opposition to Hitler. To be effective this political substance had to be couched in an artistically unimpeachable form. But the aesthetic aspect of writing was from this perspective not an end in itself. From the opposite viewpoint the writer's main task was to carry on as best he could with the kind of literary activity he engaged in before the Nazis came into power. This approach obviously implied resistance to the fascists who had banned and burned these works, but it upheld the writer's creative autonomy. Contrary to Ter Braak's insistence on total politicization of exile literature, the Marcuse school aimed at the preservation of the literary status quo with all its diversity of style, quality, and artistic orientation.

These two main camps within the emigrated world of letters coincided only partly with the main ideological division among the exiles. The notion of relegating literature to the position of a political tool was for instance entirely in line with the thinking of the Marxists. The more dogmatically Communist authors always had regarded their writing in that light, but those of a less rigid political persuasion might also agree with Ter Braak, who was himself definitely not a Communist. In opting for a totally politicized exile literature these writers took their cue from the disturbing fact that in the years before World War II the world in general seemed to condone or at least ignore Hitler's breaches of law, faith, civilized behavior, and common decency.

This tendency on the part of the world's leading statesmen and politicians to treat the Führer as if he were just another head of state made life particularly difficult for those who had fled the Third Reich. Their very existence was an embarrassing and unwelcome reminder that Germany's new rulers had forfeited their claim to the respect and confidence of other governments. In prewar days many exile writers therefore stressed the perfidy of the Nazis in order to justify themselves in the eyes of their reluctant and often downright hostile hosts.

But this was not the only reason for the many books and articles intended to expose Hitlerism for what the emigrants knew it to be. They were convinced that the Führer was not satisfied with his dictatorial rule over Germany, and they realized that he was feverishly preparing to bring first the neighboring countries, then all of Europe, and ultimately the entire world into his power. Many exile writers saw it as their duty to arouse the intended victims of Germany's imperialistic urges from their apathy. The titles of such works as Fritz von Unruh's *Europe, Awake* (*Europa Erwache*) of 1936 and Thomas Mann's essay collection *Attention, Europe* (*Achtung, Europa*) which appeared two years later left nothing to the imagination. The same purpose of alerting other nations to the dangers posed by Hitler was served by numerous reports and more or less autobiographical novels painting the horrors of Nazi Germany with its persecution and terror. Again the titles of some of the novels in this group tell the whole story, for example *Shot While Escaping* (*Auf der Flucht erschossen*) by Walter Schönstedt, published in 1934, or Heinz Liepmann's . . . *Punishable by Death* (. . . *wird mit dem Tod bestraft*) of 1935. Concentration camps provided the topic for numerous stories and reports intended to make the true nature of Nazism known outside Germany.

But for all their efforts and good intentions the authors failed to arouse world opinion against the fascists, for their works were only incidentally translated and largely ignored by publishers and public. In fact the only international best-seller of exile literature with a concentration camp setting—Anna Seghers's *The Seventh*

Cross (*Das siebte Kreuz*)—did not appear until 1942. By that time the course of events had made all warnings about the Nazis obsolete. The success of *The Seventh Cross* was largely unrelated to its political message but depended on the human interest and adventure aspects of the story.

The failure of prewar exile literature in spreading the antifascist gospel was not only due to the mixture of opportunism and fear that blinded many statesmen and a large part of the people of other countries to all signs of the German threat to themselves. The exiles undeniably also reduced their chance of arousing feeling against the fascists by putting their warnings in the form of novels and other literary genres. Not only is the reading public for serious writing too small and unrepresentative a segment of society to be capable of influencing the political climate especially in democracies; there is also an inherent tension between the aesthetic means and the hoped-for political effect. In terms of traditional aesthetics, there could even be said to exist a fundamental discrepancy. According, for instance, to Kantian thinking, artistic quality is directly proportionate to the creative work's ability to stimulate pure pleasure, free from all commitment to or interest in the practical pertinence of the expressed ideas. Such a completely contemplative attitude is of course totally at odds with the notion of political agitation, which aims at the active application of the writer's notions in public life. But it is not necessary to embrace the extreme view that the nature of literature and the demands of political effectiveness are mutually exclusive in order to appreciate the problems that the emigrant authors faced. Even almost half a century later the basic questions about the emergence of Nazism are far from settled. The victims of fascism were tragically involved in the cataclysm, and the total lack of temporal or emotional distance prevented any real insight into the larger issues. Preoccupied with only partly understood details, they lacked the comprehensive grasp of events needed for the formulation of politically effective counterpropaganda.

Many exile writers were aware of this dilemma and therefore chose to follow the path advocated by Marcuse in his polemic with Ter Braak, by avoiding direct reference to the contemporary German situation or even to the exile experience itself. But in practice even the most rigorous exclusion of political themes could not prevent the work of these exile authors from assuming topical overtones. The reason for this was already implicitly recognized in Ter Braak's admonition that exile writing should not be limited to countering Nazi literature in purely aesthetic terms. Any kind of expression of personal integrity and creative honesty inevitably had the effect of exposing by contrast the demagogy and artistic pretentiousness of Nazi literature. Therefore even the most esoteric or abstract text suggested the critical rejection of the cultural atmosphere in Germany that produced little but party line trash.

The exiles themselves by no means always saw eye to eye about the political relevance of their writing. Their widely divergent opinions became clear in the debate over the many historical novels that appeared throughout the emigration period. From Simon Bolivar to Jacques Offenbach, from Cleopatra to Mary Stuart, and from Czar Peter to Johann Strauss almost everybody who was anybody in history was grist to this particular literary mill. Soon the genre of the historical novel dominated emigrant writing to such an extent that it became the subject of heated controversy. Particularly among those who were in favor of political activism in exile literature, the historical novel found many hostile critics. They lambasted it as a vehicle for escapism and a betrayal of the emigration's responsibility and duty. The authors were accused of shunning the political realities and monopolizing the limited opportunities for publication with their irrelevant entertainments, making it still harder for the political activists to get their work in print. It was even claimed that the historical novelists were money hungry cowards who by fleeing from the challenge of the times shared the responsibility for Hitler's present and future successes.

But the genre and its practitioners were not lacking in champions and defenders. Alfred Döblin tried to explain the prominent position of the historical novel in exile literature in terms of the writers' personal situation. They lived abroad, separated from the social structure in whose fate their own lives were inextricably bound up, and no longer surrounded by their own language. At the same time they had not become integrated into the new socio-lingual field of force in which they found themsleves. Under these circumstances their urge for activity was starved of vital stimuli because a large part of the every day life around them remained meaningless for them. Excluded from the life of their own country and unable to participate in that of their place of exile, the refugees had no present on which to draw for their literary work, and so they inevitably turned to earlier times. In addition they were moved by the desire to find historical parallels to their own experiences. They wanted to define and justify their situation in a historical perspective that would enable them to reflect on their fate and try to come to terms with it.

But Döblin also saw positive, creative factors in the exile experience which made the historical novels produced under its impact very different from those written during the late nineteenth and early twentieth centuries. According to this view the previous representatives of the genre wanted to affirm and glorify the status quo. Consequently they lacked the powerful and aggressive partisanship of those who act and suffer. The exiles' inevitable political involvement on the other hand enabled them to distill the essential truth from the historical material and mobilize it in the service of their opposition to Nazism.

A more polemical defense of the historical novel came from one of its foremost exponents, Lion Feuchtwanger. In an article that appeared in *Neues Tage Buch* in the summer of 1935, he rebutted the charges leveled against the genre by claiming that past events could be presented so as to assume political relevance and topicality. "I have written contemporary novels and historical ones. After the most rigorous examination of my conscience I can declare that in my historical novels I intend to present the same topical substance as in the contemporary ones. It has never occurred to me to represent history for its own sake; in the costume, in the historical framework I have never seen anything but a means of stylization, a means to achieve in the simplest manner the illusion of reality."

Whatever impulses may in individual cases have played a role in the writer's choice of the historical novel as the preferred medium, there was also a very good general reason why the genre became so important in exile literature. The events and experiences of their own time were so traumatic to the emigrants that they were unable to gain the mental distance from it that was needed for successful creative sublimation of the subject matter. Their art was overwhelmed by reality. They tended to compensate for this by projecting their concerns onto historical topics that did not have the immediacy of the present. In this light the historical perspective was a device to free themselves from their all-too-close emotional involvement in their contemporary world. By reflecting their own fate in the past they hoped to be able to approach it with the objectivity needed to give it epic form.

4
A Year of Decision

While the emigrants were arguing among themselves about the true nature of exile literature and its contribution to the antifascist cause, Hitler pressed forward relentlessly with his political battle plan for the stabilization and expansion of his power. His first objective was the Saar territory which since the end of World War I had been administered by the League of Nations. In January 1935, in accordance with the terms of the Versailles peace treaty of 1919, a plebiscite was held to decide the future of this French-German border region. The exiled and Saarlandian antifascists of all ideological hues naturally strongly opposed the reunification of the province with Germany and spared no effort to put their case before the people. To a large majority of the population of the area, the Nazi propaganda and the apparent political and economic achievements of the new regime in Germany proved to be irresistible. The overwhelming vote in favor of joining the Third Reich forced all those who had publicly expressed their opposition to National Socialism to join the ranks of the exiles.

The free, democratic, and legal decision of the Saarland to become a German province showed that Hitler had strong popular support. It made the ineffectiveness of the exiles in opening the eyes of the world to the real nature of the fascist regime painfully obvious. Kurt Tucholsky once again drew the only correct conclusion with his observation that the Germans really wanted National Socialism and that the exiles fooled themselves with their talk about a "better Germany" that they allegedly represented. Tucholsky's extreme but justifiable skepticism had from the beginning prevented him from joining the exile cause. Now his despair became so deep that he washed his hands of Germany completely. In a letter, he wrote: "I won't have anything to do anymore with this country whose language I speak as little as possible. May it perish—may Russia conquer it—I'm through with it." And a few days before his pessimism concerning the future drove him to suicide, he found a striking image for the illusoriness of the exiles' hopes and aspirations in the face of the world's shortsightedness and indifference: "My life is too valuable to me to place myself under an apple tree and ask it to produce pears. Not me."

Valuable as his life was to Tucholsky, he gave it up rather than witness the seemingly irreversible decline of the civilized Western world. A few months after Tucholsky's suicide, Hitler embarked on the next, decisive phase of his plans for world conquest. While in the annexation of the Saar region the Nazis had triumphed by legal means, they acted in open defiance of their international obligations when early in the following year they occupied the Rhineland. The Locarno Pact of 1925 had reaffirmed the stipulation of the 1919 Versailles peace treaty that Germany was not allowed to maintain military installations or troops in the area between the Rhine and the French border. This had been the price exacted by France in return for its approval of a moderation of Germany's World War I reparations payments. As was to be expected the continued demilitarization of this region rankled in the German people. It proved to be a fruitful propaganda topic for the Nazis in their attacks on alleged traitors and enemies of the state. Hitler's decision in March 1936 to send his armed forces into the territory was therefore enthusiastically applauded by the people. In a subsequent referendum both the Rhinelanders themselves and the rest of the Germans almost unanimously approved the action.

This illegal military occupation of the Rhineland was a direct challenge to the Allies. For a while it seemed as if the Führer's daring act would provoke France to military countermeasures. It was a very tense situation in which the fascist regime itself was at stake, but in the end the Western powers backed down and accepted the accomplished fact, letting Hitler get away with his flagrant, aggressive breach of the letter and the spirit of Locarno. The failure of the democracies to call the Führer's bluff in the remilitarization of the Rhineland was due to the adoption of an "appeasement" policy toward Germany. It reflected their more or less pious belief in the dictator's basic political sincerity and in the limited nature of his objectives.

All in all the Rhineland incident once more brought home to the exiles that they were acting in a political vacuum. Neither the statesmen of the Western powers nor the German people paid any attention to their warnings that the Führer would lead Germany and the rest of the world to disaster. This sobering experience of their isolation came at a time when the literary emigration was already in a state of anxious turmoil. There was widespread and deep concern not only for the continued existence of the exile publishing industry as such but also for its political integrity. At issue was a strange and never fully explained deal between the Nazis and the leading publishing house of Fischer.

Under the terms of the agreement the German authorities allowed the firm to split into two separate branches. The Jewish owner and his "non-Aryan" employees were permitted to leave the country and set up business as an exile publisher. For that purpose the Nazis even allowed them to take along a stock of some 780,000 volumes by those Fischer authors who were banned in Germany. Gottfried Bermann Fischer was further enabled to take nearly one half of the firm's business capital and his considerable private assets out of Germany as well. After an unsuccessful attempt to settle in Switzerland, the new exile publishing enterprise was with the Nazis' blessings founded in Austria. Meanwhile the non-Jewish section of the firm continued to do business inside Germany with works and writers that were acceptable to the authorities.

The whole arrangement was highly unusual and puzzling, particularly because it involved a most uncharacteristic generosity on the part of the fascists. It could not help but arouse uneasy feelings about the new venture among the exiles who had not forgotten that Fischer played a major role in the campaign to discredit

Klaus Mann and his journal *Die Sammlung*. In view of the circumstances the ideological commitment of the new enterprise was highly suspect. This was an all the more serious concern, as the existence of the established exile presses was very much endangered by the Fischer venture. Operating on a shoestring, the original emigrant publishers would have very little chance of surviving the competition of the large, well staffed and lavishly endowed newcomer. It seems more than likely that the Nazis by agreeing to the Fischer deal also thought they were dealing a mortal blow to the genuine, politically incorruptible exile press. As it turned out "Bermann-Fischer" in due course became one of the most important and distinguished emigrant publishers. It worked in close collaboration with the Amsterdam based firms of Allert de Lange and Querido. After the German annexation of Austria the firm moved to Sweden, where it remained active throughout the Nazi period.

Indirectly Fischer's entry into the exile publishing field benefited the antifascist cause in a very different way as well, since it triggered a chain of events that led to Thomas Mann's long overdue public endorsement of and identification with the emigration. In Mann the exile establishment gained a sorely needed focal point and a widely respected and influential spokesman. His decision to throw in his lot with the refugees was all the more effective for coming so late. For a full appreciation of its impact and of Thomas Mann's extraordinary stature within the emigration it is necessary to trace his ideological development up to this point.

More than two decades earlier at the outbreak of World War I, he like many other prominent literary figures had been caught up in the wave of patriotic fervor that swept the country. He had given expression to his somewhat exalted feelings in several essays. Then his brother Heinrich Mann in a piece ostensibly dealing with the French writer Emile Zola launched a sharp attack on the intellectual supporters of misguided nationalism. Thomas quite rightly took it personally and countered with a voluminous work entitled *Observations of a Non-Political Person* (*Betrachtungen eines Unpolitischen*), in which he took issue with the spirit of cosmopolitan intellectualism and aestheticism that in his opinion was contrary to the essence of German culture. Unfortunately very few people, not even brother Heinrich, had the perseverance to read the entire work. This general unfamiliarity with the details of his arguments caused widespread misunderstandings about Thomas Mann's political views, the most serious being the notion that the novelist utterly rejected democracy as a political system. In reality he criticized only the democratization of Germany along capitalist lines "in the Roman Western sense," and the "inner annexation of Germany by the empire of civilization" as opposed to the realm of culture.

Even those who on the basis of an incomplete reading and understanding of the *Observations* accused Thomas Mann of being a reactionary nationalist should have been aware that as early as 1923 he had renounced in no uncertain terms the opinions expressed in that work. At that time he delivered a speech "About the German Republic" ("Von deutscher Republik") in which he urged support for the Weimar state, which in many ways embodied the very ideas he had attacked in the *Observations*. From this point on he left no doubt whatsoever about his political stance. Five years before the Nazis came into power, their party press already abused him in print. The fascists even then regarded him as an adversary because of his alleged francophile outlook— the same thing he himself had held against his brother fourteen years earlier. In October 1930 Thomas Mann gave a lecture in Berlin in which he sounded an outspoken warning against National Socialism and came out in support of the Social Democrats. The Nazis, knowing what to expect, had infiltrated the audience and started fights and other disruptions in an effort to prevent Mann from speaking, but he refused to let himself be intimidated and calmly finished reading his paper.

Two years later again he gave a press interview in which he declared himself strongly opposed to Hitler and his party. Around the same time he expressed his antifascist attitude in a talk before Austrian laborers in the Vienna suburb of Ottakring. The Nazis also associated Thomas Mann with the bitingly satirical political cabaret "The Peppermill" ("Die Pfeffermühle") which opened in Munich on 1 January 1933. Even though the novelist was not directly involved in this enterprise, he certainly had strong links with its leading figures. His daughter Erika directed the cabaret and together with her brother Klaus wrote most of the texts which heaped ridicule on the National Socialists.

In February 1933 Thomas Mann had been invited to address the Socialist Cultural Society in Berlin. Since he was unable to attend personally he sent the text of his speech to be read for him. Although the meeting was banned by the Nazis his connection with this opposition organization was duly noted as further evidence of his hostility toward the new rulers. In a clear gesture of defiance Mann in December of the same year, while living in a colony of exile writers in the south of France, refused to join the official German literary organization, the "Reichsschrifttumskammer." Early in 1935 Thomas Mann had once more gone on record as an antifascist with his paper "Europe, Beware," which was distributed at an international conference in Nice.

But in the minds of many, not even all these demonstrations of Thomas Mann's political viewpoint were conclusive evidence of his critical attitude toward the new regime. Among both Nazis and exiles some uncertainty remained about the firmness of his commitment to the antifascist cause. His disavowal of *Die Sammlung* and the fact that he continued to be printed and published in Germany kept such doubts alive. Mann's studied and emphatic personal neutrality and aloofness toward the emigration did nothing to convince the exiles that his heart was in the right place. Their doubts were further strengthened by the fact that even at the beginning of 1936 the German authorities, despite Mann's repeated provocations, had not yet stripped him of his German citizenship.

Under these circumstances Thomas Mann was regarded as a somewhat dubious figure in emigrant circles at the time Fischer set up shop in Vienna. On that occasion Leopold Schwarzschild as editor of the journal *Neues Tage Buch* commented that the exiled writers included just about the entire German world of letters as far as it was worthy of note. With the same ambiguity that had marked some of his earlier utterances and actions, Thomas Mann burst into print to protest this view. In doing so he may have acted out of consideration for Fischer's remaining business interests in Germany and his own stake in them. In any case at this point the Swiss newspaper *Neue Zürcher Zeitung* became embroiled in the public controversy.

In the issue of 26 January 1936, there appeared an article by Eduard Korrodi, a Swiss journalist with pronounced Nazi sympathies. He entered into the argument between Schwarzschild and Thomas Mann with the intention of alienating the novelist from the emigration and claiming him for the fascists' side. To this end he reversed Schwarzschild's claim that practically all German authors of importance had left their native soil. Korrodi asserted that the exiles constituted a worthless segment of German literature. To bolster his opinion he said that they were all Jewish and that they wrote nothing but cheap novels. Korrodi went on to contrast Thomas Mann with these allegedly inferior writers. Mann was not really in exile; he just happened to have been living outside Germany since early 1933. He was a great artist and, moreover, he was not Jewish.

Thomas Mann proved to be above this kind of flattery. In an answering letter of February 1936 he stressed the great contributions the Jews had made to German literature over the centuries. In that connection he also took issue with the fascist notion that the Jews had to be eliminated to protect the German way of life. According to Mann, Nazi anti-Semitism was really directed against the essential Christian and ancient aspects of German civilization itself. He further corrected Korrodi's statement that the exiled authors were all Jewish by reciting the names of a number of them, including himself and his brother Heinrich, who were not. Mann also addressed himself to the Swiss journalist's attempt to downgrade exile literature because it consisted largely of novels. Mann made the point that this genre was not inferior but had established itself as the leading literary form in Europe generally. The novel was far more relevant to the politically turbulent times than any other kind of writing. Thomas Mann did not content himself with rebutting Korrodi's arguments; he condemned the Nazis in the strongest terms and, adding insult to injury, taunted that for the past three years they had been unable to decide whether to revoke his German citizenship. His letter concluded with an impassioned affirmation of his own allegiance to the emigration.

There continued to be exiles who had serious reservations about Thomas Mann. Some were envious of his great reputation or presumed prosperity. Others disagreed with his political or literary orientation. But by and large his outspoken reply to Korrodi made Mann the key figure of the emigration. His reputation as a champion of the exile cause was further solidified when the Hitler regime, convinced at last that he could not be wooed into their camp, deprived him of his German citizenship. The blacklist concerned was published in December 1936, but it did not leave Mann stateless. His prominence and his friendly private relations with President Beneš had enabled him to obtain Czechoslovak nationality for himself and his family.

Later in the same month the Nazis took further action against him. The University of Bonn announced that the honorary doctorate it had bestowed on the novelist many years before had been rescinded. Thomas Mann's reaction in this instance was more pithy than his letter to Korrodi, which out of consideration for the journalist's Swiss nationality had been couched in respectful terms. Mann's response to the dean of the university opened with a reference to the "depraved powers that are destroying Germany morally, culturally and economically" and concluded with the prayer that God might help the abused country and teach it to make peace with the world and itself. The document is a deeply personal statement of position and principles. Owing to the status of the author and the vibrant conviction of his words, it almost assumed the significance of a charter for exile literature as a whole.

Of particular interest was the passage dealing with the relation between the creative and the political concerns of the emigrants. Thomas Mann did not assign priority to one over the other but spoke out for a synthesis of the two on a linguistic level: "The mystery of language is great; the responsibility for language and its purity is symbolic and spiritual, it is by no means only of artistic but also of general moral significance, it is responsibility itself, human responsibility as such, also the responsibility for one's own people, keeping its image pure before the eyes of mankind, and in it the unity of humanity can be experienced, the totality of the human problem that does not allow anyone, least of all in these times to separate the spiritual-artistic from the political-social and to isolate oneself from the latter in an elevated 'cultural' realm."

As Thomas Mann was writing his letter to the dean of the University of Bonn, the struggle between the fascists and their opponents had moved beyond the literary sphere onto the battlefields of the Spanish civil war. Armed conflict had broken out earlier in the year as the final result of political tensions that had been building up in Spain for a long time. A left-leaning republican government had legally come to power, but the country's nobility and the Roman Catholic church banded together to overthrow it and establish a fascist regime instead. Socialists and Communists united in a popular front resisted this revolution from the right.

This internal issue took on implications of much greater magnitude. Hitler and Mussolini had entered into an alliance known as the fascist Axis and decided to use the civil strife in Spain as a dress rehearsal for their own planned war of conquest. In flagrant disregard of all international agreements, they supplied the forces of General Franco, the military leader of the right-wing insurrection, with troops and equipment. The new German air force, then being built up by Hermann Goering in defiance of the Versailles peace treaty, also took part in the civil war. Under the name "Condor Legion" it used the opportunity to train its pilots, test its airplanes under combat conditions, and experiment with new strategies of air warfare—particularly the bombarding of civilian population centers.

When the involvement by the Axis was first suspected but not yet proven, the German exile writer Arthur Koestler was assigned to investigate the matter as an undercover agent for the Communist Party. In the years before Hitler's rise to power he had worked as a journalist for the big Berlin newspaper concern of Ullstein. A Communist Party member since 1931, he took his political commitment seriously enough to pass on to the Marxists the diplomatic information that he came across in his professional capacity. In 1933 he was caught at this and lost his job in disgrace. He thereupon went to Russia, where he spent almost a year before moving on to Paris. He was active in the production of antifascist propaganda literature until the Communist Party ordered him to look into the question of German and Italian participation in the Spanish civil war.

Koestler's career as a spy in Spain came to an untimely end when he happened to run into a former newspaper colleague from Berlin who meanwhile had become a Nazi. He recognized Koestler, who posed as a right-wing journalist, and tipped off the fascists. Just one hour before a warrant for his arrest was issued, Koestler managed to flee to Gibraltar. Undeterred by this narrow escape he returned to Spain later in the year on other secret missions. Early in 1937 his luck ran out when the same informer succeeded in having him arrested by Franco's forces. The incident caused a furor, and all over the world much sentiment was aroused in his behalf. Eventually so much pressure was exerted on his captors that after some three months' imprisonment he was released on the condition that he would not return to Spain again.

Arthur Koestler was but one of many volunteers of different countries and from different parts of the political spectrum who had recognized the historic significance of the conflict in Spain. They wanted to contribute their share to the fight against the totalitarianism that threatened to engulf Europe. In contrast to Koestler's cloak-and dagger activities most of those who came to the aid of the republicans did so as members of the International Brigades. These army units often bore the brunt of the military operations against the fascists. Not surprisingly the foreign volunteers included a goodly number of German exile writers. Dedicated to the cause of antifascism but frustrated by the ever more apparent political futility of their literary activity, they eagerly seized this opportunity to engage in a more direct confrontation with the enemy.

One of these literary exiles who took up arms against Franco was the novelist Gustav Regler, who ranked high on the Nazis' list of enemies. As a journalist in the twenties he had published a story that led to the public exposure and conviction of the perverted and criminal Julius Streicher, one of Hitler's oldest cronies and a prominent figure in the National Socialist movement. In 1933 Regler left the country and settled in Paris where he, like Koestler, took part in various antifascist publishing ventures. As a native of the Saar territory he also became involved in the propaganda battle that preceded the plebiscite of January 1935 and was much disheartened and disillusioned by the outcome.

In 1936 Regler, a somewhat unorthodox Communist, went to Moscow. He undertook this trip in connection with a projected biography of Loyola that was sponsored by the Party. Regler actually intended to criticize Stalin's ruthless dictatorship indirectly in his book by implying a comparison between the Russian strong man and the founder of the Jesuit order. During his stay in Moscow, Regler became aware that a political crisis was brewing involving the old-guard Communists in whose circles he mainly moved. In the middle of August the issue came out in the open with an official announcement that a number of prominent Leninists were to stand trial. They were charged with organizing and participating in the preparation of acts of terror against the leaders of the Party and the government.

This was the start of the infamous Moscow show trials that were to have ideological repercussions throughout the world. The Russian dictator was shown to resort to judicial murder of the real founders of the Soviet state in order to bolster his own absolute personal power. As a result Communists everywhere lost faith in the Stalinist version of their political gospel. Many Marxists broke with the Party but others clung to it in the desperate hope of somehow salvaging their ideals in spite of the grim and bloody realities in Russia.

Regler's reaction was typical in this respect. The trials confirmed all his worst fears about Communism, which up to this point he had hesitated to confess even to himself. He was dismayed and shocked by Stalin's callously cynical betrayal of the cause to which he had dedicated his life. Nevertheless he was not yet prepared to admit that the germ of totalitarianism was inherent in the ideological foundations of Marxism. He therefore sought to recapture on the battlefields of Spain the spirit of idealism that had originally led him to become a Communist. The Spanish civil war had broken out while Regler was in Moscow, and the progress of the conflict had been followed with passionate interest by him and everyone else as a decisive contest between the forces of good and evil. Now the military campaign seemed to offer a chance for him to cleanse himself of the corruption of Stalinist Russia. On the battlefield he might be able to atone also for his futile literary and propagandistic efforts on behalf of the Party, with which he continued to maintain a formal allegiance.

In the fall of 1936, after many bureaucratic delays and obstructions by the red functionaries, Gustav Regler went to Spain. He took with him a gift from the Communist International Writers Association for the republican forces. It consisted of a small truck, a press for printing pamphlets, a projector, and some propaganda films. When Regler had handed over this somewhat symbolic present he joined the forces that were defending Madrid against the troops of Generalissimo Franco. Gustav Regler was no newcomer to front-line action. While still in his teens he had served and been wounded in the First World War. Now he took an active part in the fighting around the Spanish capital. From that perspective he had nothing but contempt for the Communist Party officials who were attached to the republican army, for they seemed much more concerned with their own endless intrigues and power struggles than with the fate of the Spanish state.

A short time later Regler himself was appointed as a political commissar to the nationally and ideologically mixed twelfth International Brigade. (The numbering of these troop units started with eleven.) He carried out his functions in an undogmatic spirit. Rather than insist pedantically on absolute, rigid adherence to the dogmas of Communism, he used his influence to keep up the spirit of the soldiers. They certainly needed all the encouragement he could give them, since both in numbers and in quantity and quality of equipment they lagged far behind the enemy. Regler's unorthodox, humanistic faith in the power of the word manifested itself in the battle of Guadalajara in March 1937. Over the disdainful objections of militarists and Marxist stalwarts, he belabored the opposing Italian fascist troops with leaflets and rather highbrow propaganda speeches broadcast over large loudspeakers. This psychological warfare allegedly persuaded many of the fascist soldiers to defect to the republicans. In any case the engagement ended in the defeat of the revolutionaries. Three months later Regler was seriously wounded in the fighting around Huesca when a grenade hit his car, forcing the end of his active military career. When after four months he came out of the hospital he was sent to America to raise money for the loyalists.

Regler later used his personal experiences in the Spanish civil war to continue his struggle against the fascists by literary means. On his way to Mexico in 1939 he was for a while the guest of Ernest Hemingway, whom he had met and come to admire in Spain. In Key West he wrote his semiautobiographical novel *The Great Crusade* to which his host supplied a foreword. The book did not make any attempt to gloss over the tensions and frictions between the different political factions within the International Brigades. Regler also dwelt on the self-defeating dogmatic narrow-mindedness and paranoia of the official Communist Party representatives. Nevertheless *The Great Crusade* ended on a positive note. In the battle of Huesca that ended Regler's fighting days, the loyalists had scored a military victory over the forces of Franco. From a literary standpoint it was entirely justifiable to conclude the novel with this promising scene, yet in a larger context Regler distorted the truth about the Spanish civil war in closing his book on this upbeat note.

Guadalajara and Huesca were no more than retarding moments in a development that inevitably had to lead to the military defeat of the republicans. In March 1939 the fight was over and a fascist regime was established in Spain. Once again the world had ignored the handwriting on the wall. The legal government of Spain had in its hour of need been deserted by Russia no less than by the Western democracies who had failed to supply vitally important military and medical supplies and food. Some statesmen had paid lip service to the righteousness of the loyalist cause. In reality the republicans had been diplomatically and militarily abandoned by all those who refused to see the plight of Spain for what it was: the preamble to the most disastrous war ever waged. From this perspective Regler's ultimately rosy picture of the loyalist prospects in *The Great Crusade* was more than just a literary device to round out his story. It symbolized the desperate longing of the emigrant writers for some hopeful sign, some bright spot on the horizon. During six years in exile they had seen the international situation grow steadily worse. All resistance, whether with the pen or with the gun, appeared to be fruitless as the fascist scourge spread further and further. The exiles' hardship and sacrifice seemed wasted and the future more bleak than ever.

5
The Fall of Europe

The exiles' despair was further deepened by the increasing
difficulty of finding a place to live. As the years went by the
Hitler regime gradually came to be looked upon as a permanent
fixture on the political and diplomatic scene. Those who since
1933 had tried to mobilize world opinion against it were increasingly regarded and treated as undesirable troublemakers. Another
major factor in their problems was the world economic situation.
Practically all nations were in the grip of the Great Depression,
and the business slump brought with it severe social tensions that
undermined political stability. The exile press argued that the
emigrants did not, as commonly feared, weaken the economy of
their host countries, but that they actually strengthened it. But
people were in no mood to listen to reason, and the nations of the
world became ever less willing to admit large numbers of people
who had lost everything. Writers and publicists were particularly
unwelcome because it was suspected that there were many left-
wing agitators among them.

Switzerland for example came to practice an immigration policy which was so restrictive that in spite of its neutrality and
favorable location the country served as a refuge for relatively few
emigrant writers. Especially those who were Jewish—that is to
say, the majority—met with a very hostile reception. Only if
they had the necessary papers to travel on to another country had
they any hope of being admitted for a limited time, on a transit
basis. Virulent anti-Semitism was in fact rife among the top au-

thorities in the immigration department and particularly in the Alien Police.[1] In all questions concerning the entry of foreigners during the Hitler era an official policy of systematic discrimination against "non-Aryans" was practiced. The purpose of it was to "protect Switzerland from being overrun by Jews." In many instances those who in their flight from the Gestapo had succeeded in crossing the Swiss border were actually returned to the German authorities, and thereby virtually condemned to torture and death in the Nazi concentration camps.

Yet in spite of all the obstacles placed in their paths, a number of exiles found legal or clandestine ways of entering the country. But that was by no means the end of their troubles. Except for a few extremely prominent figures, even those who succeeded in being officially admitted had a very hard time earning a bare living. Their applications for employment permits were in most cases rejected. The authorities were guided in their hostile attitude by the advice of the Swiss Writers' Union, which habitually assumed a very negative stance toward exiled colleagues from abroad.

The main reason for this protectionist attitude had nothing to do with ideological questions. It was a direct result of the serious economic situation with which the Swiss men of letters themselves were confronted. Because of the extremely small German-speaking population in their own country they had traditionally depended very heavily on what they could earn from publications in Germany. With the establishment of the Hitler regime this market was virtually closed to foreign writers and journalists. Their own very shaky financial position brought about by this loss of income made them chary of the few opportunities that Switzerland offered in their professional area of enterprise. They were always mindful of the risks they would run in having to compete with the emigrants, many of whom were better known and more qualified.

The Swiss writers' preoccupation with their own material interests is clearly reflected in their advice to the authorities. The authors were usually sympathetic toward lyric poets, who rarely earned significant amounts of money with their work, and they were also fairly lenient with regard to specialists like travel authors who offered no direct competition to the native talent. In cases of this nature that did not threaten their own economic status they were inclined to recommend favorable action on entry and labor permit applications. Sometimes they even intervened on behalf of an exile in one of these categories if the Alien Police wanted to reject or expel him. In instances where the emigrant concerned posed a limited professional risk for the members of the Swiss Writers' Union, they frequently favored short term residence or work permits, or limitations on the kind of literary activity to be allowed.   ·

The Swiss literary establishment was most concerned about the journalists and publicists who wanted to live and work in their country. They were the ones who endangered the natives' own existence the most, so everything possible was done to prevent them from practicing their profession. Often value judgments and artistic criteria of dubious validity were invoked along with economic arguments to persuade the officials to refuse the necessary permits. A typical case in point was that of the Austrian essayist Alfred Polgar. He was by every objective measure one of the most talented men in his field at the time, yet the Union refused to recommend him for a work permit. It also wanted him specifically barred from ghostwriting or publishing under an assumed name, activities that out of necessity had become fairly common practice among the literary emigrants in Switzerland.

In order to justify their negative advice the Swiss professional organization defamed Polgar in almost hysterical tones. He was said to be one of those foreign authors whose literary and journalistic activity would have dire consequences not only for his native colleagues but particularly for the internal political stability of the country. A Swiss newspaper in which Polgar had published made a deposition in his behalf, stating that there was no one available to replace him as a master in his profession. The Writers' Union tried to refute this testimonial with more chauvinistic comments and the remark that it only proved the incompetence of the newspaper's management. The statement by the Union concluded with further belittling observations on Polgar's artistic and professional stature and on his alleged indifference toward the local laws. As a result of this extremely biased opinion

Alfred Polgar was not only forbidden to engage in any newspaper or broadcasting work or to give public lectures, but in addition his residence permit was limited to one year. In other cases not even such temporary reprieve was granted.

Proposed emigrant publishing ventures met with an equally unsympathetic attitude on the part of the Swiss authorities. Requests by aspiring publishers for permission to settle or work in Switzerland were in most instances denied. Their activity would in the view of the Alien Police be of no particular interest to the country; in fact it would be likely to violate its policy of neutrality. In this respect the government officials sometimes went further than the Writers' Union, with its vested interest in the availability of ample publishing opportunities, recommended. In one case of this nature the Swiss writers had proposed that the emigrant concerned be permitted to engage in business provided his enterprise did not become a typical exile venture but worked with and for the Swiss writers. The authorities opted instead for a hard line. They were afraid of provoking German reprisals if they seemed to condone or promote the production of anti-Nazi literature.

Their caution was not entirely unjustified. Aided by the local fascists, Germany's diplomatic representatives kept considerable pressure on the Swiss government to curb all anti-Nazi activities. These intimidation tactics often had the desired result. Even the established Swiss publisher Emil Oprecht ran into difficulties with the authorities over the fact that since 1933 he specialized heavily in the works of antifascist authors including many exiles. After a hate campaign against him in the local press, the Swiss Federal Council in 1937 took official action. Oprecht was warned that the government would no longer tolerate the publication of books—especially those by foreigners and immigrants—that attacked political conditions and personalities in Germany. But having made the gesture the authorities apparently were content to let the matter rest, for when Oprecht refused to be browbeaten and went right on with his antifascist publications nothing was done to force the issue.

Hostile though the attitude of the Swiss officials to the exiles often was, the country was by no means alone in its unwillingness to grant the refugees from the Third Reich asylum and let them earn a living. This became painfully obvious in July 1938. In the French resort town of Evian a conference of European and Latin American countries plus New Zealand, Australia, and the United States took place. Much publicity was given to this meeting of representatives of thirty-two nations. They were supposed to find a solution to the ever growing problem of finding a place to live for those who were driven out of Hitler Germany. All participating nations would undertake to admit as many exiles as their society and economy could absorb.

The Evian Conference raised the hopes of the hard-pressed emigrants that at last something would be undertaken to improve their lot, but they were to be cruelly disappointed. Behind the promising façade the real motives for the conference were hidden. Actually the United States had taken the initiative for the international meeting to ward off internal political pressures in behalf of the victims of Nazi persecution. Secret government directives show that the Evian Conference was set up "primarily with a view toward forestalling attempts to have the immigration laws liberalized."[2] It soon became obvious that virtually all the other countries involved were also mainly interested in keeping the emigrants out. The only result of the conference was therefore a further deterioration in the situation of the exiles. The Nazis did not waste the opportunity to score propaganda points. They gleefully pointed out the hypocrisy of the statesmen who criticized the Germans for their persecution of Jews and political opponents but at the same time were unwilling to allow these people within their own borders.

The reasons the Evian Conference had been convened at this particular time lay in the drastic increase in the dimensions of the refugee problem in the early months of 1938. It resulted from the annexation of Austria by Germany, which sent many more antifascists scrambling to get out of reach of Hitler's henchmen. This "Anschluß" as it was called had a strong private, emotional significance for the Führer. To him it was an act of revenge on his native country for not recognizing and acknowledging his genius. Immediately after he had come into power in Germany he had begun to prepare the way for his plans regarding Austria. Agitators were employed to stir up the discontent and frustration of the lower middle classes, making them receptive to the fascist promises of power and affluence. At the same time Austria's economic dependence on trade with Germany was used to exert political pressure. Austria was scarcely in a position to offer much resistance to its big neighbor. In the early thirties its only significant source of support was Italy, which wanted it to act as a buffer against possible German expansion to the south. But in return for his protection Mussolini had insisted that the Austrian government pursue a very hard line against its internal left-wing opposition. As a result Austria came to the brink of civil war and remained hopelessly divided politically. In the end the sacrifice proved to have been in vain as Germany won the Italian dictator over to its side and Mussolini dropped Austria.

Once he had weakened and isolated his chosen prey, Hitler took the next step to realize his vision of conquest and domination. In November 1937 he informed his top military leaders that he intended to protect the German people and provide for their national growth by enlarging the Reich's territory. This would obviously in addition to the rape of Austria involve the annexation of Czechoslovakia. Because of existing international pacts and treaties these actions were in turn likely to lead to war with other nations as well. The prospect of an engagement with France in particular caused the commanders of the armed forces to object strenuously to the Führer's plans, for they believed that Germany was not well enough prepared either militarily or economically to risk war on more than one front.

The military's resistance was broken through a vicious campaign of character assassination against the minister of war and the commander in chief which forced these men to resign their posts. This cleared the way for Hitler himself to assume direct control over the armed forces, making them fully subservient to the National Socialist party. Once that was accomplished, in the early months of 1938, the Nazis moved ahead with their scheme. It involved a characteristic mixture of bluff, intimidation and intrigue but met with more resistance than expected. Ideologically there was perhaps not a great deal to choose between the clerical Austro-fascism of Chancellor Dollfuß's successor Kurt Schuschnigg and the German regime. Nevertheless the Austrians on the whole did not want to lose their independence and be swallowed up by the Third Reich. Even the members of the officially banned Austrian National Socialist party were dreaming of and agitating for their own rise to power rather than annexation by Germany. Although the local Nazis were not in favor of Hitler's objectives, he nevertheless used them to pressure Austria into submission. Chancellor Schuschnigg was summoned to the Führer's alpine headquarters in Berchtesgaden, where he was forced to sign an agreement that the ban on the Austrian Nazi party would be lifted, and that the Nazis would be represented in the government.

After he returned to Vienna, Schuschnigg carried out these stipulations that meant the almost certain collapse of his regime. But he made one more last-ditch effort to save the political independence of his state. On the ninth of May he called for a popular plebiscite on the loaded question whether the Austrians wanted a free and autonomous homeland or not. The Germans immediately intervened to prevent this plan. They demanded the Chancellor's resignation and sent troops across the border to occupy the country. German Nazi administrators arrived to take over the reins of government. When the whole issue had been decided by brute force and all opposition had been crushed—in Vienna alone some 67,000 people were arrested—Hitler held his own referendum. The predictable result was that he got an overwhelming majority in favor of the accomplished fact of the takeover.

This vote was blatantly phony and meaningless as an expression of the people's real feelings on the matter. Nevertheless the Western powers used it as an excuse for accepting Austria's annexation passively. Willfully ignoring the manifest truth, they chose to regard the forcible incorporation of the country in Hitler's realm as representing the popular will. This hypocritical fiction would in years to come be used by some to cast doubt on the motivation of the Jews and antifascists who hastily fled the "Alp- and Danube-District" as Austria was renamed by its new rulers.

But for many no escape was possible. While the Nazis staged a pogrom which in extent and brutality exceeded anything that had been done in Germany up to this point, neighboring Italy and Switzerland actually closed their borders to all refugees.

Czechoslovakia too, which had until then been one of the major exile countries, one day after the Anschluß sealed itself off from both Austria and Germany. Those who managed to enter illegally were imprisoned and later turned over to the Third Reich. But no amount of kowtowing to the Nazis on the part of the Prague government could save Czechoslovakia's independence. In this case too, Hitler had been preparing for the takeover ever since he established his regime in Berlin. To this end he cleverly exploited the long-standing feud between the German minorities in the border provinces and the Czech population. The tension between these groups dated far back to the days when the entire region was part of the Austro-Hungarian monarchy. After the creation of Czechoslovakia as a separate state in the wake of the First World War, the situation had deteriorated further. The developments in Germany since 1933 had encouraged the "Sudeten Germans" to greater political activity, and in 1936 under their fascist leader Konrad Henlein they demanded autonomy.

Hitler had all along done everything he could to stir up as much trouble as possible and to intimidate the Czech authorities. As early as August 1933 he showed his utter contempt for the country's sovereignty in the Lessing affair, which was a direct threat against all anti-Nazi exiles in Czechoslovakia. Theodor Lessing, a Jew, had until 1926 held a professorship at the technological institute in Hannover, where his family had been settled for over three hundred years. He had been dismissed from his post because he published an article critical of the Weimar Republic's chief of state, Hindenburg. As a result Lessing lost his pension and his savings. He opened up a private school in his home town, but as soon as the Nazis came to power they closed it down.

Lessing then fled the country and settled in Marienbad, ten miles over the border in Czechoslovakia. But the fascists were not content to have driven him into exile. They feared his pen and also wanted to set an example for other opponents of their regime. So the Nazi party newspaper *Völkischer Beobachter* published a vicious attack on him, and at the same time the government offered a huge reward of 80,000 marks to anyone who would bring Lessing back. On 31 August 1933 two storm troopers from Munich drove across the Czech border with the intention of returning the exile to Germany. But their plan went wrong and instead of abducting Lessing they shot him to death through a window of the study where he was working. The assassins made their way back across the border to the Third Reich where they were given a heroes' welcome.

This incident set the tone for Germany's dealings with Czechoslovakia in the following years. In September 1938, strengthened by the successful annexation of Austria, Hitler moved in for the kill. He threatened Czechoslovakia that he would use armed force in order to protect the German population from alleged harassment by the majority. The Western powers saved him the trouble. Their "appeasement" policy culminated in a meeting in Munich of Hitler, French president Daladier, Mussolini, and Chamberlain. Without any consultation with the Czechoslovak government an attempt was made to placate the Führer by turning the areas inhabited by the "Sudeten Germans" over to the Reich. Because these districts were heavily industrialized their loss had very serious consequences for the Czechoslovak economy. The border region with its mountain ranges and fortifications was also the country's major line of defense. The transfer of the Sudetenland to Germany therefore left Czechoslovakia crippled militarily as well as economically.

Betrayed by its powerful allies, the Prague government found itself in a most vulnerable position. It reacted by attempting even more strenuously than before to avoid all provocation of the German rulers, which also of course meant the imposition of stern controls on the activities of the exile writers. The political atmosphere, previously fairly liberal, changed drastically, becoming in fact thoroughly fascist. As a result all Jewish writers, Czechoslovaks and exiles alike, found themselves subjected to anti-Semitic measures. Franz Kafka's friend Max Brod for instance saw his career ruined overnight. He had for many years been a leading theater critic for one of the Prague daily newspapers, but now he was suddenly forbidden to write about German plays and ordered to limit himself to the Czech stage.

Incidents like this and the presence of the Jewish refugees from the German occupied Sudetenland served as a constant reminder of what to expect once Hitler brought the whole country under his control, and there could be little doubt that he would soon do so. Although his blackmail technique in Munich had yielded him considerable territorial gains, the Führer was far from happy with the outcome of the conference. The settlement, advantageous though it was for him, had deprived him of the chance to stage a spectacular military campaign to mark his debut as commander in chief. Chamberlain had returned home from Munich with the illusion that he had achieved "peace in our time," but Hitler never had the slightest intention of abiding by the agreement.

The majority of the Jews and exiles in Czechoslovakia refused to face the increasingly obvious fact that Hitler planned to complete his conquest of the country. In spite of the Führer's track record of treachery and broken treaties, they still chose to believe his hypocritical assurances that he had no further ambitions once the "Sudeten Germans" had been brought "home to the Reich." This unwarranted faith in his words was probably not so much based on political naiveté as on a psychological inability to accept the horror that confronted them. There were nevertheless among the politically and racially endangered residents of Czechoslovakia also many who entertained no illusions about what the future held in store for them. Their fears were further deepened by the brutal attack on the defenseless Jewish population within Germany which took place shortly after the Munich meeting.

In Paris a seventeen-year-old Jewish refugee had shot a German embassy official who ironically enough was not a Nazi. On the ninth of November the fascists unleashed a nationwide wave of terror, murder, and destruction of property in retribution for this killing. It was a calculated slap in the face of the Western democracies with their "peace in our time" euphoria, but it also stepped up the war of nerves against the antifascists in exile to an almost unbearable point. As the Jewish refugees worried and mourned for the friends and relatives they had left behind in

Germany, they also had to recognize that they faced a similar fate.

Those who tried to escape the looming disaster by a timely departure for more distant parts often found themselves unable to do so. In trying to get the necessary documents together they were likely to get caught in the veritable maze of red tape with which the Czechoslovak officials did their best to prevent the Jews from leaving the country. The diplomatic representatives of the various places the would-be emigrants wanted to go added their share to the bureaucratic obstacles. The British consulate in particular, which was responsible for issuing visas for Palestine, was highly adept at delaying the administrative process.

As a result of either their own lethargy or official obstructionism, large numbers of antifascist writers were trapped when early in 1939 Hitler grabbed the remainder of Czechoslovakia. On this occasion he exploited the tensions between Czechs and Slovaks in the same manner as half a year earlier he had used the friction between "Sudeten Germans" and Czechoslovaks for his own imperialistic purposes. The Czechoslovakian president was summoned to Berlin to receive an ultimatum. He was given the choice between a military attack on his country, including the destruction of the city of Prague by bombers, and voluntary submission to Germany. The weakened country was unable to defend itself, and so almost exactly one year after the Anschluß of Austria, Czechoslovakia was dissolved into the protectorate of Bohemia and Moravia and the satellite state of Slovakia.

German troops occupied the territory without meeting any resistance, and Hitler could satisfy his desire for a triumphal entry into Prague, which he had been "cheated" out of in the preceding autumn by Chamberlain. Once again the German aggression was passively accepted by the Western powers. Apart from some diplomatic protest notes that no one took seriously, they made no move whatever to live up to the responsibilities they had assumed toward the truncated Czechoslovak state under the terms of the Munich agreement.

The spread of Hitler fascism to Austria and Czechoslovakia since the beginning of 1938 was a sinister omen for those emigrants—including almost all of the exile writers—who had settled in other countries that were within Germany's political and military grasp. Because of their dependence on the continental European linguistic and cultural atmosphere, these literary figures had at this stage only rarely made their way to other parts of the world. They tended to regard even England as being too far off the beaten track. To be sure, a number of Zionists had gone to Palestine, but they regarded that as a return from their historic exile in the diaspora. Otherwise a case such as that of the esoteric lyric poet Karl Wolfskehl was highly exceptional. Shortly after Hitler had come to power he had gone to Italy where conditions and especially the mood of the populace in these years were favorable to Jewish exiles. Then in 1938 when Mussolini at the urging of the Führer adopted an anti-Semitic policy, Wolfskehl went all the way to New Zealand. But in this particular instance philosophical and religious considerations played a part in the decision to make such a drastic break.

Apart from Wolfskehl and a very few others, the bulk of the literary emigration was concentrated in the western and northern European countries that had not yet been swallowed up by the Germans. Hitler's brazen expansionism put them on notice that their refuge might turn out to be very temporary. Therefore those who could continued their odyssey in search of a relatively safe haven. Bertolt Brecht, for instance, who ranked fifth on the Nazis' blacklist, had left Germany immediately after the Reichstag fire. After a brief stay in Switzerland he found a most congenial new home in Denmark where he spent the next five years, which were among the most productive in his entire creative career. In 1938 Brecht became convinced that Germany after its conquests in central Europe was sure to turn its attention to its northern neighbors, and he therefore moved to Finland, where he lived for one year before coming on to America.

History proved Brecht right in his pessimistic view. After the surrender of Czechoslovakia the Führer pushed ahead with his conquest of Europe. Poland was regarded as a formidable military power. Only a few months earlier it had helped Germany in the dismemberment of Czechoslovakia by annexing an important industrial region. Now it was next on the list of Hitler's territorial ambitions. Shortly after the end of the Munich meeting the Führer had already started his political offensive against the Poles by means of an unacceptable ultimatum concerning the Baltic Sea port of Danzig, which after World War I had become a free city. This diplomatic maneuver provided the dictator with the pretext he needed to launch a military operation against Poland, and in May 1939 he informed his top generals that war was unavoidable.

Hitler knowingly accepted the risk that the conflict would also involve the Western powers who had finally been shocked out of their lethargy. The fall of Czechoslovakia had caused even Chamberlain to reconsider his "appeasement" policy. Reversing his previous stand, he had promised Poland help in case of an attack. His new policy was soon put to the test. After some hectic but fruitless last minute diplomatic maneuvering, the German army invaded Poland on the first of September 1939. The Second World War had been launched. Germany soon managed to overrun the Polish army, which fought with self-sacrificial heroism but had no chance against the vastly superior equipment and organization of the invading troops. On the fifth of October, Hitler was able to review a victory parade in Warsaw.

In the attack on Poland, Germany had been supported by a new ally. A few days before the invasion the Nazis had scored a sensational diplomatic victory. While the Western democracies were still trying to come to an agreement with Stalin, the Führer concluded a nonaggression pact with Russia. For thousands of members and sympathizers of the Communist Party who had not allowed even the Moscow trials to shake their faith in Marxism, this alliance was more than they could take. Stalin had been moved by pragmatic political considerations to side with the Germans, but his reasons, no matter how weighty, were not sufficient for large numbers of Communists, especially among the exiles from the Third Reich. They refused to go along with this crassly opportunistic betrayal of the antifascist cause. The stalwarts who in spite of everything still adhered to the party line were forced by Stalin's move to change their political rhetoric. Instead of attacking the fascists as such, they now had to direct their criticism against the capitalist system generally, which meant that the Western Allies were held responsible for the world crisis.

Stalin's new partnership was particularly problematical for the German writers who had gone into exile in Russia. There were not many of them, for the Soviet Union was far from open handed with its entry permits. People who had not dedicated their life and work to the Marxist cause were almost always kept out, even if that meant certain death at the hands of the Gestapo. In fact only two emigrant authors without Communist Party affiliation were ever admitted. But even for the card-carrying comrades it was very difficult to gain admission. The Russian officials preferred them to go into exile in capitalist countries. For one thing Moscow did not trust the foreign Party members. For another, they would be more useful to the Communist cause by forming ideological cells and engaging in subversive or propaganda activities in one of the Western democracies.

Generally speaking, asylum was granted only to those refugees who were not only politically reliable but also valuable to the Russians in terms of their professional qualifications. They were employed under material conditions far better than anything any Western host country had to offer. Generous subsidies for their publications also made these chosen emigrants independent of the economic risks and limitations that everywhere else threatened the existence of exile literature. On the other hand the exiles in the USSR were in ideological bondage. They had to go along with all the curves and twists in the party line, including the German-Russian nonaggression pact. The lack of intellectual freedom in Russia, the dangerous political climate, and especially the intrigues and rivalries among the refugees themselves were obviously more than any but the most hardened fanatic could stand. Even as early as 1935 Bertolt Brecht, who was strongly committed to Marxism, cut short a visit to Moscow. His reasons certainly must have gone somewhat deeper than his own flippant explanation that he could not get enough milk and sugar for his coffee there.

The good and the bad sides of the Soviet Union as an exile country can be demonstrated with the history of the journal *Das*

Wort, which was founded in Moscow in 1936. Both *Die Sammlung* and *Neue Deutsche Blätter*, which had been the most prominent literary journals, had by this time ceased to exist. The Russian-based periodical with its generous resources immediately established itself as the leading exile publication. In the context of the then prevailing "popular front" policy of collaboration between Communists and socialists in the fight against fascism, *Das Wort* could print contributions ranging over a wide political spectrum. Articles by orthodox Marxists appeared side by side with texts from such liberal humanists as the brothers Mann. Even a conservative monarchist like the Austrian novelist Joseph Roth wrote for the journal. With the German-Russian nonaggression pact, suddenly the "popular front" policy was no longer operative, and all overt anti-Nazi propaganda had to stop immediately. The format of *Das Wort* did not fit into this new situation, and the Party decided that it had outlived its usefulness. Characteristically the journal was simply discontinued from one issue to the next. Not even the editors themselves were given any advance warning.

The friendship between the two dictators did not last long. Although Stalin faithfully lived up to the stipulations of their pact, Hitler in the summer of 1941 attacked Russia, bringing it into the war on the side of the Allies. Still the Communist writers in Moscow and elsewhere always differed fundamentally from the exile authors with other political views in their attitude toward the fascists. The Marxists looked upon Nazism as the culmination of an allegedly inevitable process of decay of Western capitalist civilization. They regarded Russia as the country that had gone farthest along the way toward a new and better form of society. Therefore they did not share in the otherwise common feeling of the emigrant authors that exile literature had the mission of preserving their cultural heritage for a better future. The Communists in fact rejected the German past along with all other capitalist traditions in favor of their visions of a dialectical-materialistic paradise on earth.

By the time the Führer's troops marched into Russia in a flagrant breach of the nonaggression pact, that agreement had served its purpose for him. It had insured him a free hand in his operations against the democracies of northern and western Europe. The first winter after the official outbreak of hostilities between Germany and the Allies had passed with hardly any military action. Then in the spring of 1940 Hitler launched his "lightning war" of massive surprise attacks with aircraft, tanks, and other mechanized forces. Within weeks or days Norway, Denmark, Holland, and Belgium capitulated before the far superior invading armies. Before the end of June, France too had surrendered to the fascists.

6
Trapped

The smaller northern and western European countries fell so quickly before the German onslaught that most of the emigrants living there had no possibility of escaping. Some were able to go into hiding for a shorter or longer time, and a few even survived that way, but most of them were captured and eventually killed by the invading Nazis. The collapse of France put the exiles there also in a desperate position, but the situation was very different from that in the other territories newly conquered by the Führer. In the first place it took him a few weeks longer to force France to submit, and even then only the northern section was directly occupied by the Germans. The southern part of the country was turned into a nominally autonomous state ruled by a pro-German puppet regime. It remained free from occupying forces until November 1942, when the Allies landed their troops in North Africa. But even though the trap did not snap shut quite as suddenly or completely as in other countries, many members of the large and active exile writers' colony in Paris fell into the hands of the Gestapo and disappeared into the concentration and extermination camps.

That the fall of France brought disaster for so many German and Austrian antifascists was the result of a complete reversal of the official French attitude toward the emigrants. Until the outbreak of the war in September 1939 France had been among the most liberal countries so far as its policy with respect to the refugees was concerned. The authorities had been relatively generous with their limited residence permits. Even when someone's "Carte d'Identité" was withdrawn it was possible to gain a considerable period of grace by launching a lengthy procedure to appeal the cancellation. As a result of this comparatively hospitable attitude France had quite early in the emigration become by far the most popular host country for the anti-Nazi exile writers.

At first large numbers of them had settled in the small fishing villages along the Mediterranean coast, primarily Sanary sur Mer. They were attracted to that region not so much because of the climate or the idyllic scenery as because life was cheap there, if relatively primitive. But before long the prospect of a more stimulating intellectual atmosphere and superior professional amenities lured most of them to Paris. The French capital became the center of the prewar emigration and the home of many emigrant organizations. One of these was an association for the protection of the exile writers' interests, which arranged many lectures and cultural events. Its programs demonstrated that France had attracted an emigrant population that was ideologically more mixed than was the case in most other host countries. The speakers ranged from the conservative Austrian monarchist Joseph Roth to the dogmatic Marxist Johannes R. Becher and included moderate liberals like Heinrich Mann as well.

Paris was also one of the very few cities outside the German language area in which German plays were occasionally staged, including some by Bertolt Brecht. The emigrant press developed very considerable activity. Among many other titles *Das Braunbuch über den Reichstagsbrand*, a collection of documents about the Reichstag fire edited by Willi Münzenberg, was published there. The editor's claim that the book sold some 600,000 copies in two years and was translated into thirty-three languages needs to be taken with a grain of salt. Even so the *Braunbuch* was undoubtedly one of the very few international best-sellers produced by the exiles. Paris was furthermore the center for a most unusual publishing venture which specialized in "camouflaged" literature. Antifascist political pamphlets and also some literary texts by authors whose works were banned in Germany were bound in covers of travel guides and cookbooks or even disguised as packages of tea. The idea was that in this way these publications could be sent to Germany and distributed throughout the country by mail without being detected by the authorities.

Undoubtedly of greater practical significance was another exile enterprise based in Paris, the journal *Neues Tage Buch*. It was the continuation of a highly reputable periodical called *Tagebuch* which dealt with economic issues. It had been published in Berlin until it incurred the wrath of the Weimar Republic's rulers for its sharp criticism of their policies. At that point the whole operation was moved to Munich so as to get away from the Prussian authorities that harassed the editor in Berlin. In its new locale *Tagebuch* did not of course survive the "parallelization" of Bavaria. Editor Leopold Schwarzschild was forced to leave the country, and four months later in July 1933 he entered the arena of exile publishing with the first issue of *Neues Tage Buch*. It was financed by Dutch capital, a circumstance that would later enable the journal to survive somewhat longer than other emigrant publications based in Europe.

The strength of *Neues Tage Buch* lay in its extremely skillful and penetrating analyses of the economic condition of Germany. Based on what little information could be gotten from inside the country or gleaned from official statements and documents, the journal revealed how the Nazis were manipulating their finances in preparation for war. *Neues Tage Buch* soon became an indispensable source of information for leading political, administrative, and business circles throughout democratic Europe. The Nazis were visibly disturbed that many of their schemes were brought to light by Schwarzschild and his small staff of experts.

Whatever its political value, all this activity was far from lucrative, and on the whole the exile writers in France as everywhere else except Russia had a hard time making ends meet. Even a man as well known and hard working as journalist and novelist Joseph Roth was in constant financial trouble. Although in the view of other emigrants he managed to extract more than his fair share of royalties from the exile publishers who handled his books, and had further income from translations, lectures, and other endeavors, much of his correspondence consisted of begging letters to his various acquaintances. Stefan Zweig, in particular, who could easily enough afford it, helped him often with financial donations. But it was a vicious circle. The hardship and humiliation that Roth endured drove him to drink more and more, and his galloping alcoholism increased his living expenses while reducing his earning potential. Soon Roth no longer saw a way out of his private and professional impasse, and his drinking became consciously self-destructive. In May 1939 he died in a pauper's hospital in Paris.

Roth's early death at least spared him the new anguish and indignity inflicted on the exiles when war was declared and the French authorities suddenly changed their status into that of "enemy aliens." A few days later, allegedly at the recommendation of some of their French colleagues, they were interned. Along with all other German and Austrian refugees the writers were herded into an open-air bicycle stadium on the outskirts of Paris. It lacked even the most basic amenities to accommodate the twenty thousand men who had been rounded up. After ten days they were transferred to camps in the provinces that offered even fewer facilities.

Besides physical hardship the internees were subjected to torturing uncertainty about their prospects. Officially the purpose of the internment was to check the political reliability of the exiles to make certain that there were no Nazi agents among them. This explanation was not very convincing because everyone had been investigated several times already. Moreover, none of the known profascist Germans residing in France had been taken into custody. In any case no further examination of the refugees' ideological integrity was in fact undertaken. It may be assumed that the entire action served the primary purpose of diverting the French populace from the country's lack of military preparedness by playing on its latent xenophobia and anti-Semitism.

The exile writers had sacrificed their existence and careers to the struggle against fascism. Now they found themselves identified with their mortal enemies under the motto "boche est boche." They were deeply hurt and disillusioned by this sudden hostility on the part of the country that many had adopted as their spiritual and emotional home. Eventually, as the initial winter of the war passed without a German attack, the first panic among the French abated and the exiles were released again. But the experience had made it only too clear that their prospects in France had become very dim and uncertain. Many of them therefore tried to find a new and safer place of refuge.

The whole of Europe was now in such immediate danger of being overrun by the Germans that for the first time the literary emigrants out of necessity became interested in North and South America as possible destinations. But it was difficult to obtain the necessary papers and the administrative processes involved were very time consuming. As a result only a few exiles actually succeeded in leaving the country—and the European continent—before the beginning of the German offensive on the western front in early May 1940.

At that point the French immediately interned the exiles again. This time the women as well as the men from sixteen to sixty-seven years of age were rounded up. The rapid advance of the German army caused fear and panic among the captive anti-fascist exiles. They were even deprived of the possibility of fleeing for their lives. Frantic attempts were made to persuade the camp commanders and the French authorities to release them so that they might at least try to evade capture by the Nazis, but all the exiles' pleas were denied. The closer the German troops came, the greater the chaos in the camps and the confusion among the officials. Yet until the very end the guards in the concentration camps had orders to shoot anyone trying to escape.

Thus the exiles, who by their opposition had incurred the fascists' hatred, were condemned to await passively the arrival of Hitler's henchmen. Cornered in this way, more than a few committed suicide as the only possibility of avoiding an even worse fate. Others preferred the risk of being shot by a French guard over the certainty of falling into German hands and tried to break out of the camps. Some French commanders did in fact close an eye to such escapes, and in some instances the officials at the last minute tried to evacuate the internees ahead of the German army. The total confusion among the French officials, the disruption of rail and road transportation by German air attacks, and the chaos created by masses of fleeing civilians turned such attempts into yet another nightmare for the emigrants.

After the surrender of France the situation in the northern part of the country occupied by the Germans was of course particularly dangerous for exile writers who were wanted by the Nazis, but those who had been interned in the south or somehow had managed to make their way there were not much better off. Under the terms of the armistice the puppet regime in Vichy was obliged to turn over to the Germans anyone the Nazis wanted. It was therefore of vital importance to stay out of the hands of the French police. This was no easy matter since most emigrants virtually lived on the streets and in the cafés and the authorities made constant checks and raids aimed at all those who did not possess every one of the requisite papers and permits. Moreover, although this section of the country was not really occupied, German patrols were known to be on the lookout for people wanted by the fascists.

The ever present danger of being arrested and imprisoned or handed over to the Germans made the seemingly endless delays that the exiles encountered in their efforts to obtain the necessary travel documents particularly traumatic. Their time and money rapidly ran out as they made the rounds of the various consulates, mainly located in Marseilles, from which they hoped to get the papers on which their very lives depended. They were faced with an almost impossible task. In order to continue their quest for a safe asylum the emigrants needed not only a passport but also, since virtually the only available ships sailed from Lisbon, transit visas for Spain and Portugal. Furthermore, an exit permit from the French authorities was required, which was not issued unless the refugee was in possession of the Spanish visa. All these documents could be obtained only by those who held an entry permit issued by the country of destination.

Since the stateless exiles had no possibility of getting a valid passport, they were dependent on receiving a visa from the United States of America, an exceptional document in that it also served in place of the normal personal identification. A considerable number of these American visas were eventually issued through the intervention of the Emergency Rescue Committee. This organization of prominent exiles and influential Americans recommended potential recipients to the Presidential Advisory Committee and the State Department.

Even if an American or other entry visa could be arranged, the exile still had to overcome other scarcely less formidable hurdles. All the necessary documents, including an additional exit permit for those trying to get out of occupied France, had to be valid at the same time. This caused endless problems because all of these papers expired a very short time after they were issued, and it was impossible to predict how long each of the consulates involved would take to provide their respective documents. Frequently the French also delayed the issue of an exit permit for someone who had finally gotten all his transit and entry visas in order, until the other papers were no longer valid. Often the only help for the emigrants caught in this lethal red tape came from the various American committees that had undertaken the task of providing financial relief and assistance in dealing with the bureaucrats. Especially the Quakers exerted themselves on behalf of the exiles, but even their dedicated efforts were often of limited usefulness in the face of the complexities of the situation.

Under these circumstances the refugees clutched at any straws. In the spring of 1941 five ships were scheduled to sail from southern France to America by way of Martinique. The prospect of avoiding the problem of getting Spanish and Portuguese visas enticed many exiles to stake their luck and their last money on these sailings. In order to secure passage on one of these vessels one needed not only a ticket but also a security deposit of 9,000 francs, a French exit visa, a permit to land in the Antilles, and an entry paper from the ultimate country of destination. In addition, those headed for Central or South America had to have a document allowing them to pass through the United States.

Most of the emigrants who even in the face of these financial and administrative demands succeeded in booking passage on one of these ships were in for a sad surprise, for only two of the vessels reached their destination. One was forced to end its journey at Trinidad and the other two got no farther than Casablanca, where the passengers were again interned under extremely harsh conditions in desert camps by the hostile French officials. Finally after four months those who survived were allowed to continue on their way to America.

However, not all the difficulties encountered by the exiles in their frantic attempts to escape from the Nazis were due to bureaucratic obstruction. Alfred Wolfenstein, for instance, a lyric poet of note, fell victim to his own life-style. He tried to leave Paris just before the German forces occupied the city, but the last bridge over the Loire was blown up at the very moment he reached the bank of the river. The secret police then arrested and imprisoned Wolfenstein, but for unexplained reasons he was released again after three months, whereupon he went into hiding. In this situation it was particularly difficult for the rescue committees working on his case to get him out of the country. Finally at the end of 1940 it looked as if everything were set. The necessary visas and the financial guarantee had been provided for him by a prosperous Brazilian, the brother of the woman with whom Wolfenstein was living. But even before the documents were in the poet's hands, he had changed his domestic situation and set up house with another woman, which invalidated all the complex preparations that had been made for his rescue. Wolfenstein managed to elude the Nazis for years by hiding in barns and stables in the south of France, and finally returned to Paris under an assumed name. When the city was liberated in 1944 he was taken to a hospital for the treatment of a serious heart ailment contracted during his years on the run. But it was too late. Early in 1945 he committed suicide in a fit of depression.

Even aside from cases like that of Wolfenstein where unforeseeable circumstances prevented rescue, it was quite impossible after the fall of France to get more than a small percentage of the trapped exiles out of Europe legally. In spite of the danger of getting caught, large numbers of emigrants tried to enter Spain illegally in order to escape from the Nazis and reach safety, but the border guards and patrols were only the first of the obstacles they had to overcome. No less formidable was the physical challenge of crossing the Pyrenees by night on hidden and often barely passable paths. The difficulties were such that volunteers had to guide the refugees. The seventy-year-old Heinrich Mann, one of several exile writers who made their way to Spain in this manner, later pointed out that the steep trails he had climbed were "really meant for mountain goats, not for an author of advanced years." Still he did make it over the border and eventually to America.

Others were not so lucky. The noted essayist and philosopher Walter Benjamin was caught while trying to get into Spain. A professorship was waiting for him in the United States, but when his escape attempt was foiled he committed suicide, as did others under similar circumstances. Even after crossing the Pyrenees there were still many hazards to be faced before the exile could board a ship in Lisbon. The Spanish and Portuguese police were unpredictable in their attitude, and an even greater danger was posed by the German secret agents who were especially active in the capital of Portugal. On several occasions they went so far as to kidnap prominent antifascists who were awaiting their departure for a safe refuge overseas.

The journalist Berthold Jacobs for instance ranked high on the Nazis' blacklist. Early in the Hitler era he had fled to Switzerland, but German undercover agents had abducted him from Basle and forcibly taken him to Berlin. The Swiss government protested this violation of its sovereignty and did succeed in having Jacobs returned to Switzerland. In 1940 he was among the many emigrants who tried to reach the United States via Spain and Portugal. He succeeded in making his way to Lisbon but there was again captured by German secret police and transported back to the Reich, where in 1943 he was tortured to death.

Compared with the exiles who found themselves in the path of the German army in its lightning campaigns in the spring of 1940 or experienced the humiliating and traumatic conditions in southern France, the emigrants who had taken up residence in England did not fare so badly. Although the British Isles never became a major center of exile literature, a number of refugee writers had settled there in the years before the war. Among them were such prominent figures in their own respective fields as the vitriolic essayist Kurt Hiller, the formidable Berlin theater critic Alfred Kerr, and the internationally popular short story writer Stefan Zweig. England had never been a particularly good market for German literature, and there was virtually no publishing activity in their own language by or for the exile writers there. On the other hand in each of the immediate prewar years on an average more than a dozen works by antifascist emigrant authors were published in English translation, which indicates a considerable degree of interest in the political aspects of exile literature among the British reading public.

After the outbreak of the war thousands of German and Austrian refugees in England were interrogated by screening committees that divided the emigrants into three categories. Some were able to convince their questioners that they were indeed bona fide opponents of the Nazi regime, and as such were allowed to go on living and working unhindered as before. Others who did not make quite as positive an impression were provisionally left free but could at any time be taken into custody in the interest of national security. Finally there was a small group of emigrants who for some reason aroused the suspicions of the committees. They were placed in concentration camps that were, to be sure, civilized enough in comparison with those in Germany or even in France.

When in the summer of 1940 it looked as if Hitler might try to invade England, the British changed their policy toward the emigrants. All German and Austrian refugees regardless of their previous classification were summoned to report for internment. Most of them were released again two years later when the danger of a German invasion appeared to have passed. In the meantime a number of the exiles were temporarily held in camps in Canada and Australia. Though the emigrants received relatively humane treatment from the British, their already very limited opportunities for literary work were totally disrupted by their internment. Their confinement to camps not only made it physically impossible for them to write and publish, it also made it painfully clear to them that they were total outsiders of the society in which they had sought refuge. As authors and publicists they were no less relentlessly trapped in the vacuum of isolation than their personally harder pressed compeers in the cheap hotels and consulate waiting rooms in Marseilles.

Exile writers who escaped from the nazified continent of

Europe to more remote parts of the globe were professionally no better off either. Especially if they stood at the beginning of their literary careers at the time of their emigration they had little chance of pursuing their vocation. The best they could usually hope for was an occasional contribution to some emigrant journal that could pay little or nothing for it. As the example of Paul Zech, a promising young poet who had no way of realizing his creative ambitions in Argentina, indicates, German literature was deprived of some interesting talents in this way.

From 1934 till 1946 the significant liberal-humanistic journal *Deutsche Blätter* appeared in Chile. In Mexico, which harbored many Communist exiles, the Marxist emigrant publishing house Das Freie Buch was founded. But the existence of these enterprises on the whole made little difference to the unfavorable conditions that prevailed in Central and South America for the exiled antifascist authors. It was the exception that proved the rule when novelist Anna Seghers in her Mexican refuge succeeded in writing the best-selling concentration camp story *The Seventh Cross*. And the situation in the more distant or exotic host countries from Turkey to Hong Kong was even less propitious than in Latin America.

Excursus

7
The Other Side

The exiles' problems were of course noted with great glee by the Nazis who had driven them out of Germany in order to silence them as writers. Still it was not enough for the fascists to denounce the emigration and gloat over its misfortunes. They also had to provide an alternative German literature. The leaders of the Third Reich were very much aware of the importance of literature as a factor in political life. Authors who, out of conviction or opportunism, were prepared to wield their pens in the service of the fascist "new order" could count on official support and encouragement.

The propagandistic value of literary fame was demonstrated in the case of dramatist Gerhart Hauptmann.[1] The onetime Nobel Prize winner was practically the only truly renowned writer to throw in his lot with the Nazis. In the year before Hitler's rise to power, Hauptmann's seventieth birthday had been celebrated internationally with much pomp and circumstance, confirming his position as a literary world figure. In retrospect it is clear that his unassailable prominence in the realm of German letters was not really based on the artistic quality of his works. Aside from a unique sense of the theatrical, he was a mediocre writer whose manuscripts required extensive editorial revamping before they could be published at all. Hauptmann was moreover intellectually insignificant and lacking in spirit.

It was precisely these negative qualities, the lack of substance and personal engagement, of his writings that accounted for his success. Not being committed to any ideological or artistic standpoint, he could adapt to every fashionable trend and style. This flexibility enabled him from the beginning of his career in the late nineteenth century to remain always in the forefront of literary developments. By the time of World War I he had already become so popular that the progressive qualitative deterioration of his gigantic output could not affect his status any longer. His reputation as a poet of great compassion and social consciousness was based on some of his early naturalistic plays. It was never shaken later by the opulence of his way of life. Although he drank the entire proceeds of his 1912 Nobel Prize in one wild summer on the Italian Riviera, he continued to be revered as a champion of the poor and oppressed.

As Hauptmann grew older he tried more and more to emulate Germany's great classical poet Goethe in behavior and appearance. Although the irreverent poet Else Lasker-Schüler remarked that he looked more like Goethe's grandmother, Hauptmann did succeed in establishing himself as a national myth. In the twenties this process was further stimulated by the spirit of the times. As a socialist-gone-bourgeois the dramatist personified the very essence of the Weimar Republic. He immensely enjoyed his public role and had no intention whatever of risking the sumptuous life-style that it entailed for the sake of principle or politics. He put himself and his popular image immediately at the disposal of the Hitler regime when it assumed power in 1933, and the Nazis used the vain old man to impart some glamour to what was left of literary life in Germany after the exiles had departed. The most festive occasion in this respect was Hauptmann's eightieth birthday in 1942, which was marked by great public celebrations and the appearance of books and articles dealing with his personality and work. Ideologically loyal literary historians discovered in his writing the epitome of National Socialist art.

All this wassail and jubilee could not obscure the reality that Gerhart Hauptmann was a relic of the past. For all his fame he contributed nothing toward the maintenance of an active, viable literary life on a respectable level of achievement in Nazi Germany. The new regime was consequently faced with the task of promoting the kind of writing it wanted and needed for its own purposes. How much importance the Nazis attached to this matter may be gauged from the speed with which they acted. Through the takeover of such existing bodies as the Prussian Academy for the Arts and the creation of new administrative structures, the party assumed full control over the mechanics of literary life.

But all organizational measures were of little use without the right kind of manuscripts. When he gained power Hitler himself had publicly proclaimed his ideas on the role of art and writing in the Third Reich. In a speech given on the occasion of the first National Socialist party diet in September 1933, he announced the "heroic" doctrine of "blood and soil." He vehemently condemned as decadent and essentially non-German the progressive, experimental, and cosmopolitan currents that dominated the literary and artistic scene especially in Berlin. Artists and writers were assigned the task of expressing the soul and the creative potential of the people as a whole in its Teutonic purity, uncorrupted by "civilization." This term in Nazi usage had a very negative meaning, comprising Marxism, nihilism, democracy, internationalism, Judaism, and all other forces that Hitler held responsible for the decline of the West.

The fascists did not need to start from scratch in their endeavors to build up the kind of literature that would meet the Führer's criteria. Some writers had been practicing something quite like it ever since the end of the nineteenth century. A good example of this proto-Nazi writing was the work *Rembrandt as Educator* (*Rembrandt als Erzieher*) by Julius Langbehn. It was first published in 1890 and by the outbreak of World War II had gone through some hundred editions. In this tremendously popular book almost all the elements of fascist party literature could already be found. It included the antiurban back-to-the-country theme, chauvinism, anti-Semitism, confused metaphysical speculation, and the cult of health and vigor so dear to the fascists' hearts. All this was purported to be exemplified by the seventeenth-century Dutch painter as a prototype of the Nordic genius.

Other writers from the turn of the century onward produced novels that in their preoccupation with specific rural areas and their use of dialect also anticipated important aspects of the Nazis' literary ideals. Richard Wagner must also be mentioned in this connection as author of the textbooks for his operas. They consisted largely of adaptations or imitations of motifs and elements from old Germanic sagas, with heavy emphasis on racial purity and on the alleged glories of the Teutonic past.

These various forerunners provided fertile soil for the literature of National Socialism. From the mid thirties onward numerous works appeared that exploited one or more of the themes favored by the fascists. Generally speaking these books fell into four broad categories. The first of them dealt with war, usually World War I. These novels sentimentalized and glorified the experience of front-line action. A model for much of this kind of writing was found in the war diaries of Ernst Jünger, which were published as early as 1920 under the title *In Storms of Steel* (*In Stahlgewittern*). By his glorification of war and his fervent advocacy of total mobilization for the purpose of a political revolution, Jünger did much to prepare the way for the Hitler dictatorship. Nevertheless by the late twenties, before the Nazis had gained power, he severed his relationship with them because they were not ruthless and radical enough to suit him. From the viewpoint of his implacable resentment against democracy, Jünger accused Hitler of relying too much on "democratic-Western maneuvers" in his pursuit of power, and demanded an uncompromising power grab.[2]

Notwithstanding his ideological inclinations Jünger was a skillful literary craftsman, and few if any of the later books in this vein came anywhere near his level of stylistic competence. But the crudeness both of form and content of the run-of-the-mill war epics did not stop them from becoming highly popular. In 1934 one of them was made into a successful movie called *Shocktroop 1917* (*Stoßtrupp 1917*). The original title of the novel *Faith in Germany* (*Glaube an Deutschland*) reveals the reason for the public's interest in this literary genre. It helped gloss over the national humiliation of the lost war of 1914–18 by presenting it as a glorious and heroic chapter in Germany's history. This approach supported the Nazis' claim that the country's defeat and subsequent troubles were the work of traitors at home and abroad and so prepared the people psychologically for a war of revenge.

Other writers went further back into the past in order to find illustrations of the essential greatness and valor of the German nation. The old Icelandic sagas were particularly popular as literary subject matter. These wild tales of the deeds and adventures of the Scandinavians who settled the arctic island from the end of the ninth century onward were either retold or imitated by many writers in the Third Reich. While in the war novels the superiority of the Germans was demonstrated in direct armed confrontation with "lesser" people, the Nordic theme prudently avoided matching its Germanic heroes with other Europeans.

The war epics had to resort to some crass distortions of historical reality in order to boost the readers' national self-esteem. The contemplation of the Nordic people's mythic greatness did away with the need for obvious falsifications. The geographic and chronological escapism of this genre was specifically a reaction against Germany's failure to achieve any of its objectives and ambitions in European and world politics since the beginning of the nineteenth century. Hans Friedrich Blunck, the Nazi who became president of the literature section of the Prussian Academy for the Arts when Heinrich Mann was removed from that post, was a prominent representative of the Nordic school of writing.

The most typical form of Nazi literature and the one which made the greatest impact on the reading public was that associated with the "blood and soil" cult. Basically it was also escapist, but unlike the nordic genre it did not invoke ancient Germanic tribes to provide an idealized contrast to the alleged decadence of modern civilization. Instead the writers concerned found their models of all Teutonic virtues closer at hand among the German farmers of the present and the recent past. Like the war experiences and the spirit and substance of the old Icelandic sagas, the rural realities were also sentimentally idealized and distorted.

Confused mysticism and metaphysical reflections were standard ingredients of the "blood and soil" literature. Its practitioners almost to a man hailed from the lower middle classes. On the personal level their work was a defensive, antagonistic reaction against the intellectual and cosmopolitan way of life from which their humble origin and level of education excluded them. Their social class formed the backbone of the National Socialist movement, which derived its momentum from the same frustrations and resentments. The private flight of these authors into a falsified and romanticized rural primitivity was therefore at the same time an expression of the fascists' fundamental attitude toward social and philosophical matters.

Like the war novels and the saga adaptations, the "blood and soil" works were marked by at least a pretense of artistic and conceptual profundity. No such veneer of literary respectability was affected by a great deal of verse and a number of stage pieces that were intended purely and simply as party propaganda. This type of writing included inspirational songs for marching blackshirts, rabidly crude anti-Semitic texts, and paeans to Hitler. The quality of these products was without exception execrable. Even the Nazi officials were sometimes embarrassed by it and tried to find excuses for the inability of these semiofficial party bards to write anything of even modest literary merit.

The Nazis' concern for the quality of the writing produced under their aegis was, especially in the earlier years of the regime, motivated by the desire to give the lie to the view that all talent had gone into exile. Hitler Germany was eager to project an image abroad of a country in which the arts flourished. The regime wanted to cover up the relentless repression of all oppositional writing. Works that toed the party line too obediently were by definition of no use in this connection, so the authorities tolerated a certain amount of literary activity that did not conform too closely to the official ideological and artistic dogmas.

The fascists could afford to permit the production and distribution of this kind of literature because it was in essence politically neutral. It kept aloof from the problems and the issues of the times and concentrated instead on the individual's soul, on lofty eternal values, and on aesthetic preoccupations. This thoroughly escapist attitude also expressed itself in the frequent choice of historical themes and other topics that lent themselves to generalization and introspection.

A typical example was Ernst Wiechert's novel *The Simple Life* (*Das einfache Leben*) which appeared at the outbreak of the Second World War. The very popular book told the story of a naval captain who withdraws to the country to spend the remainder of his days as a fisher and hunter, contemplating nature. Travel descriptions were also much in demand, especially those in which a Greek setting enabled the author to blend current myths of Germanic glory with the traditions of antiquity. Paralleling a prominent trend in the out-and-out party literature, novels with a World War I setting formed another major category in this "inner emigration" school of writing. These works invariably suppressed the distasteful aspects of carnage and horror and concentrated instead on the protagonist's private world of exalted values and ideas.

After the war the writers concerned would vociferously protest their antifascism. They claimed that their outwardly nontopical works fueled anti-Nazi sentiments among the German population through oppositional and critical allusions that were too subtle for the censors to detect. An obvious flaw in this argument is that the fascist authorities did not assign their most illiterate people to the task of controlling literature. Any political heresies too well camouflaged for the Nazi watchdogs to find would certainly also pass by the average reader.

Nevertheless, especially in the first years, there was indeed a tendency to make defiant gestures cloaked in highly ambiguous language in novels, book reviews, and essays. In Werner Bergengruen's story *The Great Tyrant and the Lawcourt* (*Der Groß-tyrann und das Gericht*), for instance, the most outspoken comment is contained in a description of the weather, which may or may not hint at Hitler's Austrian origin and the corrupting effect of Nazi rule on the people.

And indeed, still in the morning hours that evil wind that blows from the south-east, humid and hot, began to dominate. The air became hazy, the sky was covered with pus- and lead-colored veils whose layers the treacherously and slowly stinging sun vainly tried to penetrate. Some said of this wind that invisibly it bore the minute spores of a poisonous desert plant. However that may be, it is certain that it brings about changes in the state of mind of many people. In some it causes a paralysis of their powers of decision-making, in others of their judgment; in the one bad temper and anxiety, in the next an excessive and ostentatious self confidence. In many it arouses an irregular urge for activity, others it destines for disgruntled idleness. Here it results in physical discomfort, there in confusion of soul and conscience, and even a stern judge regards it as an extenuating circumstance if an act of wildness, passion or revolt was committed during the time of this wind. However it also extends its uncanny power in bringing certain people to a bold, even shameless openness; it bring hidden things to light and allows that which man kept locked away within himself, or had forgotten, to rise up tempestously. In short, it transports all those who are open to its influence—and there are many of them—in some way or other beyond their own normal selves.

Those among the reading public who were privately opposed to the new regime developed in their ideological and intellectual isolation a particularly keen eye for any such ambiguities and possible critical allusions, though in most cases they read more into the text than it really contained. Ernst Jünger's highly successful novel *On the Marble Cliffs* (*Auf den Marmorklippen*), for instance, documented the "hero's" withdrawal into a fictitious, utopian world of his own making. But because of its conceptual obscurity the work was frequently regarded as a parable of anti-Nazi resistance.

In actual fact the literature of the "inner emigration" served the interests of the ruling powers. It provided an emotional safety valve for their antagonistic subjects who were thereby diverted from the idea of concrete political resistance. The readers who belonged largely to the educated middle class found spiritual refuge in the ideal universe evoked in these novels, which gave them a kind of soothing mental massage that helped them reconcile themselves with the harsh realities of life under Hitler. The idea of resignation in the face of adverse political conditions had strong roots in Germany's most hallowed religious and philosophical traditions. Both church reformer Luther and Enlightenment thinker Kant demanded the people's unqualified submission to whatever temporal authority happened to be in command. The influence exercised by the "inner emigration" literature was all the stronger because of the cultlike devotion with which the leading authors in this group were regarded by their large and faithful reading public.

The ambiguous ideological position of this literature extended to some of the writers themselves. Ernst Jünger, for example, took a courageous private stand against certain aspects of the fascist regime. Ernst Wiechert too, who in his immensely popular works preached passivity and introspection, did not lack personal strength of character. He publicly supported the outspokenly antifascist theologian Martin Niemöller and as a result had to spend some time in a concentration camp. Yet a writer like Jochen Klepper was probably more typical of the "inner emigration" movement.

In his private life Klepper displayed the same spirit of resignation and the same tendency to escape from the realities into a metaphysical realm as in his writings. Because he was married to a Jewess, after 1933 he lost his editorial job and was subjected to harassment and persecution. In 1937 he published his novel *The Father* (*Der Vater*) which dealt with the mysticized history of the Hohenzollern dynasty. Its success gave him a brief respite from the fascists' hostility, but later in the same year he was expelled from the official writers' organization, an action that virtually barred him from all literary activity. With the outbreak of the war he joined the army, which was often regarded as ideologically neutral, but very soon he was dismissed again. His professional and social ostracism made life increasingly difficult for him.

When toward the end of 1942 one of his adopted daughters was about to be taken to an extermination camp for Jews, he could bear it no longer. Together with his wife and daughter Klepper committed suicide, but even this desperate ultimate step was not taken in a spirit of rebellion or protest against the forces that had ruined his existence. In spite of his harrowing experiences he had no quarrel with the National Socialists. In his fiction and even more directly in his diaries he subscribed to an attitude of passive acceptance and acknowledgment of the prevailing political situation.

No less paradoxical than Klepper's acquiescence in a regime

that hounded him and his family to death was the position of those writers who were basically in sympathy with the "new order" in Germany but nevertheless went into exile. The translator and essayist Rudolf Borchardt for instance was a former member of the exclusive and esoteric circle around the charismatically autocratic lyric poet Stefan George. He had transferred his enthusiasm for the "Führer principle" from the literary realm to the political sphere. He regarded strong-man Hitler with admiration and also approved of many other aspects of Nazism. Even so he was forced to leave Germany and join the antifascists in their exile because he was a Jew.

A borderline case was that of the prominent and prosperous Austrian author Franz Werfel. He detested the Nazis but had been in favor of the totalitarian trends that developed in his homeland before the Anschluß. The leading figures in Austria's ruling clerical-fascist clique were among Werfel's acquaintances, and he has been called a friend of the Austrian variety of the fascist corporate state.[3] His experiences as a refugee did not change his rather feudal views. In 1944, for instance, he published an essay about the sanctity of property in which he denounced old age and health insurance as a fiendish by-product of base materialism. His political stance was probably based on his social and aesthetic predilection for pomp and circumstance rather than on any clear ideology. In any case he, like Borchardt, as a "non-Aryan" had no choice but to emigrate.

In these instances the racial discrimination practiced by the Nazis overrode any personal preferences and left the authors concerned no alternative but exile. Yet there was no manifest need for novelist and journalist Bernard von Brentano to live outside Hitler's Germany. This racially pure scion of an old noble German family was, especially in the early war years, a dedicated National Socialist and a fanatical anti-Semite. Nevertheless he chose to reside in Switzerland, where he lived on the periphery of the exile community. At the same time he maintained close relations with the press and cultural attaché of the German embassy. After the fall of the Third Reich he explained that his association with this official had been merely a protective façade, although it was of course also possible to see it in a more sinister light. But whatever ambiguities attended Brentano's private circumstances, his writing throughout this period and into the postwar years was consistently fascist in tone and tenor.

Much more complex in this respect was the case of Josef Breitbach. In 1919 he had become a French citizen; in the early twenties he lived in the south of France and from 1929 onward in Paris. On the one hand he helped the antifascist literary exiles who settled there, financially and in other ways. On the other he distanced himself publicly from the "hate-propaganda of rootless emigrants and their journals" and even tried to persuade the French publishers to print pro-Nazi works rather than exile literature. Later he changed his attitude, siding with the exiles in their opposition against Nazism and contributing to one of their journals. And he was by no means the only, nor the most prominent, figure to reverse his stand. As the result of a similar development from pro- to anti-fascism, some of the leading men in the Hitler movement ended up in the camp of the exiles.

Hermann Rauschning played an important role in the Nazi organization. During 1933 and 1934 he served the regime as National Socialist senate president of the Free City of Danzig, then he became disillusioned and resigned his post. In 1936 he fled to Switzerland and from there went to the United States. He built a distinguished academic career and published several inside-story accounts exposing and denouncing the Führer. Another convert to antifascism had been even more deeply involved in the Nazi movement. At one point Otto Strasser had even become a serious rival of Hitler in a power struggle within the party.

In the twenties he had worked hard as a publicist and party functionary to build up a strong National Socialist organization in northern Germany. Up to that time the fascists had found very little support in that part of the country. But Otto Strasser's efforts were too successful. He and his brother Gregor acquired such a strong and loyal personal following in the region that the Führer felt his own authority threatened. Hitler also disapproved of Otto Strasser's insistence on taking the socialistic planks in the Nazi platform seriously. The party's relations with its backers in big business were jeopardized by Strasser's support of strikes organized by the trade unions and especially by his demand that the party endorse the nationalization of industry.

In the fall of 1925 it looked as if the Strasser brothers were getting the upper hand in this power struggle. They even won over Josef Goebbels, who at a party meeting denounced Hitler as a petty bourgeois and demanded that he be ousted from the party. But the Führer was politically more astute than his opponents, and early in the next year he maneuvered the brothers into a position in which they had to acknowledge his leadership. Nevertheless conflicts and tensions continued to exist between them. When Hitler in May 1930 demanded total submission on the part of the brothers, Otto Strasser refused to comply. He was then expelled from the Nazi party and founded his own truly socialistic organization, the Union of Revolutionary National Socialists. But this "Black Front," as it was generally called, failed in the elections held in September of the same year to make any serious inroads into the Nazi vote. In 1933 Otto Strasser went into exile and from that time on wielded his pen against Hitler, who deprived him of his German citizenship in November 1934.

There were also turncoats who first opted for the exile cause and then as the years went by and it became clear that the Hitler regime was not going to collapse any day soon, reconsidered and changed sides. A fairly typical example was the writer Grete von Urbanitzky, who left Austria at the time of the annexation in 1938 and spent two years in the emigration. When the victorious German troops occupied Paris, where she had taken up residence, she contritely renounced that episode and returned to Vienna. The most spectacular case of defection from the antifascist camp was that of Ernst Glaeser, who had established his considerable literary reputation with the autobiographical novel *Birth Date 1902* (*Jahrgang 1902*). In the Weimar Republic he had incurred the hostility of the right-wing elements, who initiated legal action against him because of his allegedly sacrilegious publications. Before he left Germany in November 1933 he had completed the novel *The Last Civilian* (*Der letzte Zivilist*), which dealt critically with the history of the Nazi movement.

His attitude toward the publication of this work had already raised some doubts about his commitment to the antifascist cause. While still in Germany, Glaeser had concluded an agreement with an exile publisher who was in the process of establishing himself in Paris. In spite of this binding contract the author subsequently also offered his manuscript for publication to a number of other publishers both in and outside of Germany. In order to protect his interest the exile publisher had to let it be known that the book was under contract with him. When Glaeser's association with the antifascist emigration had in this manner been revealed, he no longer felt safe in Germany and went into exile. Afterward he tried to force the publisher to pay him advances by threatening that otherwise he would return to Germany.

Against this background it was not surprising that he was not very well liked or trusted by his fellow exiles, who also found it suspicious that the Nazis had banned only those of his books that had been written before 1933. Furthermore Glaeser's expressed view that "insecurity is the writer's true element" was regarded as an ideological escape hatch to justify a possible sellout to the National Socialists. The suspicions against Ernst Glaeser were strengthened in September 1937, when an article by Joseph Roth appeared in the Parisian exile publication *Neues Tage Buch*. Roth reported that a "mediocre German writer who for incomprehensible reasons was in the emigration" had refused to publish in one of the most prestigious exile journals because some of the other contributors were Jewish. Although Roth had not specifically named him, Glaeser issued a denial, which under the circumstances had the opposite effect.

In any case his subsequent actions established beyond a doubt that Roth's story had hit the nail on the head, at least so far as Glaeser's true feelings were concerned. He became involved in some political intrigues spun by the Nazi clique in Zurich; then in May 1938 he returned to Germany where he soon became editor of the fascist army newspaper *Adler im Süden*. But even with this total about-face he had not yet reached the limit of his adaptability. Shortly after the end of the war he published an article in which he heaped praise on exile literature, calling it the "conscience of the nation that had long warned in vain" and that had preserved the word. At the same time he obliquely tried to justify his own unprincipled opportunism by crediting the people who had chosen to share the fate of Germany with "Tolstoyan patience."

Glaeser was not the only writer to display such remarkable versatility in the face of changing political conditions. As the Third Reich collapsed, Russian and Polish troops drew close to Gerhart Hauptmann's home in the Silesian mountains. To ingratiate himself with the prospective new masters, he had Russian and Polish translations of his works hastily put on display in the castlelike mansion. And after the foundation of the German Democratic Republic, the eighty-four-year-old writer wasted no time in howling with the new wolves. He formally promised culture minister Johannes R. Becher to undertake the "tremendous task" of putting himself at the service of reconstruction, saying he aspired to become an example for the population in the entire Russian occupation zone. Only his death soon thereafter saved him from this final indignity. Instead his corpse was made to serve the Marxist propaganda line in a series of macabre ceremonies held throughout the country, at one of which he was praised as "one of those German prophets to whom it was given to lead their people out of the darkness into the shining light of Communism."

II:
1939–1947

8
America as Asylum

While in Germany the Glaesers and Hauptmanns were arranging themselves with the Nazis, trading their personal and artistic integrity for comfort and security, the exile writers found themselves ever more hard pressed in their search for a sanctuary from fascism. After the conquest of Europe by Hitler, America had become the only hope for many of the antifascists trapped by the German army. It soon developed into the main center of exile literature.

Yet the United States proved to be anything but a country of unlimited opportunity for the emigrants. During the prewar days when the Great Depression with its tremendous unemployment and poverty determined the political mood of the country, the State Department kept a very tight lid on the issuance of immigration visas. In 1934 as the true nature of the Nazi reign of terror became obvious, President Roosevelt called for generosity on the part of the officials concerned. His directive was almost totally disregarded by the consular officers overseas.

It was not until the wholesale massacre of Jews and destruction of their property by the Nazis in the night of 9 November 1938, that public opinion became mobilized. A Gallup poll conducted at the time found that 94 percent of the people disapproved of the treatment of the Jews in Germany, but the noncommittal nature of such expressions of popular sentiment became clear from an inquiry conducted by the business journal *Fortune* only a few months later in April 1939. On that occasion 83 percent of those interviewed were against the admission of more immigrants. Nevertheless under the impact of the atrocities of the "Night of Broken Glass" ("Kristallnacht"), the President could politically afford to cut through some of the red tape concerning the immigration policies. He ordered that twelve to fifteen thousand German refugees who had entered the country with visitor's visas would have their papers extended for six months and not be expelled after the documents expired.

The real test of the official American attitude toward the refugee problem came with the fall of France. The German conquest of Europe put great pressure on the United States, and on the whole the Washington government failed to meet the challenge. Through procrastination and bureaucratic intrigue it frustrated most initiatives for the rescue of the victims of Hitler's racist policies until 1944, and by then it was too late for most of the Jews and other "inferior" people. Only when the end of the war was already in sight were energetic measures taken to save the lives of those who had not been exterminated yet.[1]

While the refugees in general received scant help and comfort from the United States, writers and other public figures on the whole fared much better. Special arrangements had been made for them immediately after the French capitulation in the summer of 1940. Between one and two thousand people in this category, including relatives, were enabled to escape to America. This action was initiated by the Emergency Rescue Committee, a private body founded by American authors. The influential journalist Dorothy Thompson and popular historian Hendrik van Loon played particularly prominent roles in this organization. The major figures among those exiles who were already in the United States or South America—such as Thomas Mann, Hermann Kesten, and Stefan Zweig—collaborated closely with their American colleagues. Working through the President's Advisory Committee, the Emergency Rescue Committee nominated recipients of "emergency visas" of which the State Department somewhat reluctantly made a limited number available.

Once in the United States, the exiles were confronted with social and cultural conditions that were utterly foreign to most of them. They were faced with numerous problems of personal and professional adjustment, one of the major difficulties they experienced being that of reconciling reality with their preconceived notions about America. As typical European intellectuals their attitude toward the country was highly ambivalent. On the one hand they were convinced that it was sadly lacking in civilization and was a hotbed of unbridled capitalism, while on the other hand they still indulged in the traditional European idealization of America and its institutions.

Novelist Hermann Broch for example, who later with *The Death of Vergil* (*Der Tod des Vergil*) was to write one of the weightiest works of exile literature, had even before the establishment of the Nazi regime in Germany expressed his view of America as the cradle of progress. Broch's three-part novel *The Sleepwalkers* (*Die Schlafwandler*) written in 1931–32 dealt with a topic that had a very rich tradition in German literature: the emergence of a "new man." But in contrast to the mythological grandeur with which Nietzsche tackled the subject in his *Zarathustra* and also contrary to the exclamatory pathos of expressionistic versions of the theme, Broch's approach could be characterized as historical speculation. On the basis of established trends, he projected the development of a new, objective-minded kind of human being out of the romanticism and chaos of the past. According to one commentator this fundamental thesis was not only exemplified in the various heroes and antiheroes of the story, it was also placed in the context of a comprehensive philosophy of history through the choice of the settings in the different parts of the novel.

The successive scenes of the action are generally located farther and farther to the West, a progression reflecting the philosophical evolution from Eastern mysticism to occidental rationalism in which mankind is allegedly caught up. In the course of the trilogy the background of the actual plot moves from Berlin to a French village on the banks of the Moselle, as humanity gradually frees itself from the fetters of irrationalism. The ultimate aim of this development is indicated in an extension of the geographic symbolism. The protagonist of volume two is fascinated with the New World, regarding the United States as a land of freedom and justice and the birthplace of mankind's beckoning future.[2]

These were exactly the ideas that during the preceding two

centuries had lured large numbers of German immigrants to America. They accounted for the existence of an established German-American population of more than five million. Having come to the United States at different times for a variety of religious, political, economic, and personal reasons, these people and their descendants formed a by no means homogeneous social element. The large majority of them by now had little or no emotional attachment to their original homeland. The only German-Americans still vitally interested and involved in German matters were those belonging to the conservative urban and rural middle class. These people tried to preserve their cultural heritage in nostalgic imitations of the life-style of the "old country." The image of Germany they tried to evoke was inevitably that of a bygone age—a romanticized vision of the good old days as seen from a lower middle-class or rural viewpoint.

Its essentially reactionary outlook made this sector of the German-American community highly susceptible to the lure of Nazism as a movement allegedly aimed at the restoration of Germany's past glories and virtues. From 1933 on, this affinity with fascism was clearly reflected in the development of the German societies. Until then these organizations had been virtually apolitical. Traditionally 20 to 25 percent of the membership had consisted of Jews, and until the establishment of the Hitler regime in Germany these people were never discriminated against by the "Aryan" members. From 1933 onward the atmosphere changed more and more until most German societies were blatantly anti-Semitic, which soon forced the Jewish members to withdraw.

Obviously then the German-American element among the American population was either basically indifferent or downright hostile to the antifascist cause. It was therefore of no help whatever to the exiles who were trying to find their feet in the United States. Matters were made even worse by the fact that the German societies were by no means the only or even the most important centers of fascism in America. Long before Hitler's rise to power a small but rabidly fanatical Nazi movement had sprung up, organized by fascists who after the failure of Hitler's attempted coup in Munich in 1923 had fled to the United

States. Since at that point they had little success in infiltrating the established German-American societies, they started their own organizations. These soon merged into two nationwide federations: the Landesgruppe USA of the National Socialist German Labor Party, whose membership was open only to German citizens, and the Friends of the Hitler Movement, for American sympathizers. After Hitler had taken over the reins of government in 1933 these two organizations were combined under the name Friends of New Germany.

During the late thirties the Nazi movement flourished exceedingly under the aegis of the German-American Bund. By the time war broke out in Europe it had reached a total of some 2,500 regular members with about ten times that many sympathizers, distributed over fifty-five local branches. The Bund's activity culminated in a mass rally held in Madison Square Garden in February 1939, complete with fist fights between Nazi thugs and left-wing exiles. Dorothy Thompson contributed her share to the melee by laughing derisively at the fascist speakers until she had to be rescued by the New York police. In addition to the Bund as the central Nazi organization, there were also dozens of pro-Hitler groups operating under the guise of bookstores, societies, leagues, bureaus, alliances, associations, offices, and services of one kind or another.

The emergence of fascist trends was not solely due to the official and unofficial propaganda efforts by the Germans. Extreme right-wing and totalitarian tendencies surfaced in American society generally, possibly even in such a phenomenon as Roosevelt's charismatic personal leadership.[3] On a lower level the parallelism between political developments in Europe and America could be seen in the case of Huey Long. As governor of Louisiana from 1928 to 1932, and then as a United States senator, he displayed distinctly Führer-like ambitions, promoting a cult of blind admiration and loyalty among his followers.

Such fascist tendencies in the United States were triggered or at least stimulated by the Great Depression. This also applied to the heightened activity of the Ku Klux Klan, which served as the model for similar racist organizations that sprang up all over the country. The example of the Nazis directly inspired the political

career of William D. Pelley who founded the Silvershirt movement. Pelley claimed that in a deathlike trance it had been revealed to him that there was an international Jewish plot afoot
against the United States. According to his alleged mystical
source of information, the road to salvation lay in the trans-
formation of the country into one enormous business corporation,
which was to be headed, not surprisingly, by William D. Pelley.
In spite of this blatantly self-seeking nonsense the Silvershirt
movement soon numbered some fifteen to twenty thousand uni-
formed, armed, and trained members. Similar groups of mili-
tants and Nazi sympathizers also attracted many followers in all
parts of America.

The fascist currents in American politics were only the excesses
of a very widespread ideological move toward the right. This
general trend also affected the views of those German refugees
who had come to the United States in the early and middle thirties before the writers and publicists started to arrive in any significant numbers. Until 1938 or 1939 it was mainly Jewish
business people, scientists, and scholars who had chosen America
as their place of exile. The first mentioned category was by
and large politically neutral or conservative from the beginning.
Among the intellectuals who were driven from Germany there
were many who came to America as supporters of socialist and
other left-wing ideologies. In the course of their exile they often
changed over to the other side of the political spectrum.[4]

This move to the right determined the changing attitude of
such prominent scholars as the sociologist Hannah Arendt and the
members of influential institutions like the New School for Social
Research and the Institute of Social Research. The New School
had originally been established in a sociopolitically progressive
spirit, but since 1923 it had under Alvin Johnson's leadership
assumed an increasingly more conservative character. Nevertheless in the middle thirties Johnson set out to recruit many of the
left-wing scholars who were then emigrating to the United States
from Europe. With a characteristic mixture of open-mindedness
and opportunism, he used this available and relatively inexpen-
sive talent to start a high-powered graduate program. Very soon
the foundation members of the faculty of this so-called Universi-

ty in Exile adapted themselves to the general rightist atmosphere of the New School. Renouncing their own political past, these emigrants strenuously opposed the hiring of other progressive professors. In particular the economist Emil Lederer, a former socialist, was very active in his endeavors to keep exiled scholars who did not share his newly adopted conservative views out of the University in Exile.

At first this conservative attitude caused considerable tension between the New School's graduate faculty and the "Horkheimer Circle," as the Institute of Social Research was usually called. But soon Max Horkheimer, the founder and guiding spirit of this organization, and his coworkers also abandoned the radical left. Horkheimer himself became skeptical and disillusioned with politics generally. Other members of the Institute of Social Research veered rapidly to the right and before long represented an extreme conservative position.

Leo Lowenthal for instance moved so far away from his original radical socialist ideas that in 1949 he was appointed director of the research department of the Voice of America. Karl A. Wittfogel, who before his exile had been the China specialist of the German Communist Party, was soon recognized by the American authorities as a leading expert on Asian affairs, and he eventually became an enthusiastic supporter of the fanatical red-baiting Senator Joseph McCarthy. Wittfogel allegedly even denounced as a Communist the "sponsor" who had enabled him to find refuge in the United States.

A comparable if less extreme swing to the right also took place in the theological circles around Paul Tillich, who until 1933 had been the leading representative of "religious socialism" in Germany. Like Horkheimer, Tillich soon after his arrival in America distanced himself from his earlier convictions. He now rejected the idea of a religiously based social-critical engagement in favor of an essentially individualistic outlook. Undoubtedly in his case, as in that of Horkheimer, practical considerations played a certain role in the change of views. Obviously, socialist ideas of any kind were not acceptable to the majority of Americans as an alternative to the traditional political concepts.

Among the antifascist journalists in American exile a shift

from left to right was in some instances also noticeable. The former editor of *Die Neue Weltbühne* William S. Schlamm provides a case in point. During the summer of 1938 he had left Czechoslovakia at the last moment before the borders were closed. After brief sojourns in Brussels and Paris he reached New York in the middle of November, where he immediately started to contribute to the exile press in America. In his very first publication he still stressed his adherence to the cause of socialism. He claimed that it would bring the devastation and destruction of human civilization to an end by acknowledging freedom, dignity, and self-determination as the highest values. And it was not only with regard to such ideal abstractions that Schlamm at the beginning of his American exile subscribed to socialism, for in the same article he also endorsed its central doctrine—according to which the most important means of producing material goods had to be transferred from the ownership of a few privileged families to that of a solidary society.

Only a few months later, in February 1939, the first sign that Schlamm was already beginning to revise his political ideas appeared. In some instances he still seemed to accept the orthodox Marxist view on war as a phenomenon of decaying capitalism, while at several other points he ironically rejected these theories. Several months later Schlamm gave evidence that he had completely freed himself from the concepts and dogmas of leftism. Going to opposite extremes, he for instance no longer regarded Nazism as an outgrowth of the extreme right wing but rather as a social revolution dressed up in conservative slogans.

There was a direct connection between Schlamm's political turn to the right, which before long led him to conservative extremes, and his quite uniquely successful career in American journalism. From the beginning of his exile he made a concerted effort to establish relations with the American press. As soon as he felt enough at home in the English language he virtually severed his connections with the exile press. In 1941 he was invited to act as adviser on European affairs for the prominent business magazine *Fortune*. He proved himself and his grasp of American conditions with a lengthy feature article about the situation of the blacks in the southern states, which was published in *Life* under the title "The Negro's War." Partly on the strength of this work, Schlamm in the fall of 1941 was appointed as assistant editor of *Fortune*. A year later he was promoted to senior editor.

Schlamm soon drew the attention of the founder and publisher of *Time*, *Life*, and *Fortune*. Henry R. Luce was greatly impressed by his journalistic talent and especially by his articulate expertise on matters pertaining to European politics and economics, and early in 1943 Schlamm became Luce's personal adviser and assistant. As such he enjoyed considerable prestige and influence in the most prominent publishing enterprise in the country, if not the world. He established close personal and professional ties with such rabid anti-Communists as Whittaker Chambers and William C. Bullitt who were also associated with Lucepress. Schlamm's unbridled admiration for Senator Joseph McCarthy as the chief anti-Communist "witch-hunter" confirmed his total political about-face.[5]

A right-wing bias manifested itself also in certain political activities of the exile community. In this respect the emigrants from Austria could do more than those from Germany because the United States never recognized the Anschluß. Consequently when America entered the war the Austrians were not classified as "enemy aliens" and were not subjected to the inhibitions that this status imposed on the Germans. The relative prominence of the conservative element on the Austrian exile scene was in part due to the presence in America of Otto von Habsburg, the pretender to the throne of the Austro-Hungarian monarchy which his father Karl I had lost at the end of World War I.

In the spring of 1940 Otto had fled from his residence near Brussels just one jump ahead of the German army. Spurred on by his mother, the politically ambitious former empress Zita, he tried to use the exile movement for his own ends. He hoped to exploit the concentration of many central European emigrants in America to regain a position of leadership among his dynasty's former subjects. Such restorative tendencies found little echo among the diverse non-German-speaking national groups that had formed part of the Austro-Hungarian monarchy, but the

American authorities did at least for a while acknowledge him as the leading figure among the Austrian and eastern European exiles.

For a long time Washington supported Otto's main project, the formation of an army battalion of Austrian exiles which was to fight side by side with the Allies against the Germans, somewhat along the lines of the Free French forces. Although Habsburg undoubtedly also pursued his own political aims and ambitions with this project—he insisted on designating himself as commander—it also had its perfectly legitimate justification. There were precedents both in the First and Second World Wars, but the planned Austrian battalion was of particular symbolic significance. Since Federal President Miklas at the time of the Anschluß in 1938 had chosen to remain in the country, no legal government in exile could be formed. The national army unit would under these circumstances have provided the only possible basis for the formal recognition of Austria's continuing sovereignty by the Allies.

As early as April 1939 the novelist Joseph Roth declared in France that the organization of an Austrian military unit should have top priority. Without it all other activities on behalf of the country's future would, according to Roth, be doomed to ineffectiveness. In September 1940 a number of prominent Austrian exiles urged the British government to allow the formation of an Austrian legion. In America President Roosevelt personally supported the idea until the Russian victory at Stalingrad made it politically inopportune. Roosevelt would have been satisfied with a token battalion of company strength, in other words one hundred and twenty men.

This seemed modest enough in view of Otto von Habsburg's propagandistic claim that he could recruit five thousand volunteers. It was a very realistic number even in the light of his official guarantee to the Washington authorities that he would be able to provide eight or nine hundred men. At the beginning of 1943 the recruiting drive was finally opened, but during the following three months Otto succeeded in signing up only twenty-five volunteers. Because of this debacle the project was dropped and Otto von Habsburg was thoroughly discredited politically.

This development gave great joy to the left wing of the Austrian emigration, which naturally reveled in the loss of face suffered by the conservative leader. The Social Democrats had furthermore traditionally been in favor of the unification of their country with Germany, and they were not particular about the way it was brought about. Even Hitler's Anschluß was welcomed by them as a realization of their ideal. They wanted to perpetuate the Führer's forcible merger of the two countries. The socialists had therefore all along strongly opposed the battalion that would symbolize Austria's autonomy. They made the most out of the project's failure.[6]

Contrary to the left-wing propaganda line, the lack of volunteers did not indicate the bankruptcy of the conservative element among the Austrian exiles. The decisive reasons for the fiasco lay in the fact that a large number of the young immigrants had already been drafted into the United States forces. Moreover, hundreds of men between thirty-five and fifty who offered their services for the Austrian battalion had to be rejected because of an age limit set by American army regulations. Recruitment was further inhibited by the consideration that due to the legal complexities of the situation in case of capture by the Germans, members of an Austrian military unit would have been regarded and treated as traitors rather than as prisoners of war.

The setback that the conservative cause suffered through the failure of the Austrian battalion did not affect the basic political bias toward the right among almost all sectors of society. The conservative trends among the American population and the bulk of the antifascist emigrants created a widening ideological gulf between the general public and the exile writers. But the literary emigration was not only alienated from those who identified with the political right. Between the fall of France and Pearl Harbor the exile writers also isolated themselves from the other left-oriented refugees and the American socialists. The cause of this lay in their positive attitude toward the question of American intervention in the war. The extreme left was normally and as a matter of principle against participation in the armed conflict. From a dogmatically Marxist viewpoint it was a manifestation of the decay of the capitalist system to which both sides belonged.

Less radical socialists also tended to be against the entry of America into the war. Their attitude was based on ample historical evidence that such military involvement would inevitably strengthen the cause of conservatism. They were afraid that the country's participation in the hostilities would spell the end of the progressive New Deal era, and events proved them right. As late as 1940 Norman Thomas as the leading exponent of socialism in the United States was also the most prominent pacifist. Both leftists and rightists among the German emigrants were moreover afraid that American intervention in the war would endanger their often very precarious new existence. They foresaw that under war conditions they were likely to be designated as "enemy aliens." This indeed happened with President Roosevelt's proclamation of 8 December 1941, which applied to "all natives, citizens, denizens or subjects of Germany, not actually naturalized."

There was another reason as well for the anti-intervention attitude of many emigrants, including those from the left. As a neutral state America could maintain diplomatic relations with Germany. These contacts could be used for the rescue of victims of the Nazi regime. The United States did in fact have consular representation in Germany until June 1941, and until October of the same year the Nazi authorities under certain conditions allowed the emigration of Jews. The participation of America in the war would mean the end of their last legal opportunity of eluding the fascist henchmen by emigrating to the United States. Last but not least the exiles were concerned that by endorsing the widely unpopular idea of intervention in the war they would themselves lend momentum to the antiemigrant and anti-Jewish currents in America.

For all these reasons the exile authors as socialists and Marxists should really have been against American intervention in the war. In fact, however, they came out in favor of it because their particular interests apparently overrode general political considerations. Many other emigrants had given up the idea of ever returning to their own country, but the writers were altogether too much a product of the German language and the cultural climate of central Europe to renounce their origins. It was essential for their existence and their work and it was the aim and the purpose of their exile that the Hitler regime be defeated. They realized that this goal could be achieved only with the aid of America's military resources. This politically uncharacteristic attitude of the exile writers prompted William S. Schlamm early in 1939 to the observation that it was a paradox of the times that the political left manifested "warlike pathos" while the right was more inclined toward "defeatist pacifism."

When America eventually did take up arms against Hitler and his allies, it was as a result of Roosevelt's policies and Pearl Harbor and not in response to the writers' "warlike pathos." Their attempts to inflame the public's passions against the fascists were as fruitless in the United States as they had been everywhere else. It is not surprising that under these circumstances a paralyzing sense of futility could overcome even the most dedicated among them. Ernst Toller, for instance, admitted defeat in his long journalistic and literary struggle against fascism. He committed suicide in New York in March 1939, a few months before the outbreak of war. Toller enjoyed a considerable political and literary reputation. He had played a leading role in the short-lived Communist government established in Munich at the end of the First World War and had spent five years in prison after its collapse. After 1933 Toller became very active in the political life of the emigrant community. He used his great popularity as an author and public speaker to propagate his view that the writer in exile was duty bound to devote his talents to the political struggle for freedom and humanity. Purely creative and aesthetic ambitions had to be sacrificed to the aim of opposing Hitler through propaganda and politically engaged writing.

As an acknowledged spokesman for the activistic, aggressively political anti-Nazi segment of the literary establishment, Toller had defined his view of the writers' exile as early as 1933 in a defiant open letter addressed to propaganda minister Josef Goebbels. In this document he had stressed the crucially important role of the exiled author as the guardian of true German culture in the struggle to defeat National Socialism. Toller had in this context avowed that the fascists' hatred and persecution would strengthen the exiles' determination. In the course of the following years, he represented the same vehement and assertive brand of antifascism in numerous publications and public speeches.

Until the end Toller apppeared in public with his customary air of alertness and confidence. A few days before his suicide he attended a White House reception for exile writers, but privately he complained of being tired and unable to find any rest. It was spiritual rather than physical exhaustion that caused him to seek oblivion and escape from the frustrations and disappointments of his existence in death. He was scheduled to travel from New York to London but insisted on discussing the question of suicide with the friends who helped him pack his suitcases. The following morning he worked in his New York hotel room as usual. While his secretary was out for lunch he hanged himself in an adjoining bathroom.

This act of despair was naturally grist to the propaganda mill of the Nazis, who had always maintained that the emigrant authors were doomed to utter ineffectiveness and had no political or professional prospects. The fascists' gloating made Toller's self-destruction an all the more painful debacle for the exiles themselves. They could only regard it as a betrayal of everything they stood for and a clear capitulation by the leading activist among them. But in their emotionally charged condemnations of Toller's suicide, the emigrants really only attempted to hide from themselves the fact that he had every reason for despair and resignation. Hitler seemed increasingly in command and was apparently permitted by the Western powers to rape and pillage the rest of Europe at will. Also Toller could not have helped becoming skeptical about giving speeches and writing articles for a public consisting mainly of fellow exiles. They shared his general outlook, although maybe not his activist philosophy, but were at best tolerated guests in their places of refuge, and as such, politically isolated and powerless.

The extent of Toller's isolation and the lack of resonance of his ideas were revealed with shocking clarity on the occasion of his cremation. Only three people attended: the emigrant author Ludwig Marcuse who was probably Toller's only close personal friend in the final phase of his life, a distant cousin who was hoping for a legacy, and an American woman journalist with whom Toller had had an affair. As a final irony his actress wife could not be present because on that same day she opened in Los Angeles in a production of the classical German playwright Schiller's drama about the medieval Swiss freedom fighter William Tell.

Toller's suicide signaled the bankruptcy of the idea that exile literature had to be no more than a means to a political end. Even before the outbreak of World War II reduced all warnings against Hitler's thirst for power and conquest to utter redundancy, the activist school of emigrant writing had fallen victim to its inherent inconsistencies. It had been based on the misconception that a literary movement could successfully oppose modern totalitarianism. Instead, as Toller's case proved with poignant clarity, the voice of warning had spent itself crying in a desert of indifference, opportunism, and hypocrisy. The exile authors who subordinated literature to the direct resistance against Hitler had not succeeded in becoming the intellectual leaders of a global antifascism. They were ignored or regarded with suspicion as fanatical troublemakers who tried to spoil the dream of "peace in our time."

The beginning of armed hostilities in Europe and especially Pearl Harbor relieved the exile writers of their Cassandra role. From that time on they tended to take a broader view of the rise of fascism, placing it in a larger historical framework. In this context the more perceptive authors could not fail to realize that Western civilization would never again recapture its former spirit and grandeur. Even after the defeat of Hitler, the barbaric fascist interlude and the experience of total war would mark a definitive break with those values that had evolved over the centuries in Europe.

To those not blinded by ideological doctrines, the awareness that the old way of life was a thing of the past could be extremely traumatic. It implied that the self-imposed task of preserving the German cultural heritage was doomed to futility. Therewith the painful exile experience had lost its purpose. Even though the exiles might be able to return to Europe after the war, their spiritual and intellectual homeland was lost forever. This prospect was difficult to accept for these people who were both personally and creatively wholly conditioned by their national traditions.

The internationally famous author Stefan Zweig for example could not cope with the loss of the world in which he had lived.

Zweig had already once before tasted the bitterness of exile. During the First World War he had taken up residence in Switzerland. In the spring of 1934 the Austrian police searched his house in Salzburg. The presumable reason was the writer's close friendship with some members of the socialist party, which at the time was embroiled in a conflict with the authoritarian regime of Chancellor Dollfuß. It was to be another four years before fascism in its more brutal, German variety would spread to Austria. Still the incident was sufficient to persuade Zweig that for him as a Jew, a cosmopolitan writer, and, as he was fond of saying himself, a person of "eminently pacifistic" attitude, the handwriting had appeared on the wall. Although it was not yet absolutely necessary, he unobtrusively left his country. He severed his connection with his German publisher and went to London, where he stayed until 1940. Then he took up permanent residence in Brazil, from which he made frequent visits to the United States.

Owing to his inherited fortune and to the worldwide success his books had for many years enjoyed, Stefan Zweig was in a very favorable position among the exile writers so far as his financial resources were concerned. His wealth enabled him to maintain his habitual air of the hypercivilized man of letters. Somewhat superficial and glib in his conversation and manners, he seemed more interested in the latest gossip from the literary world than in any political issues. This impression was accurate to the degree that Zweig did indeed keep aloof from anything that smacked of politics. He was especially careful to keep himself out of the vicious conflicts between the different exile groups.

But the impression of imperturbable good humor that Zweig consistently made even on his best and closest friends was misleading. Ever since the beginning of his exile he had felt that the events in central Europe signaled the final collapse of the world and the civilization in which he belonged and without which he could not and would not live. The eclipse of this "World of Yesterday," as he called it in the title of his posthumously published autobiography, was to him more than the end of a historical era. It deprived him of his existential basis and reduced him to a sterile relic of bygone days.

This emotional crisis was further aggravated by the professional problems inherent in the emigration to which even Zweig was not quite immune. He worried much over his creative future and toyed with desperate and impossible plans to adapt his writing to the loss of his natural German and Austrian public. His new dependence on the Anglo-Saxon world with its very different tastes and norms in literary matters perturbed him deeply. Zweig was moreover unable and unwilling to delude himself about the possible role of literature in the conflicts and struggles that were shaking the world to its very foundations. Unlike so many of his fellow exile writers, he had no illusions about the power of the word against terror, barbarity, and brute force. And so he often felt that the pursuit of a literary career had become futile and irrelevant. In 1942 he reached the end of his capacity for hiding his profound, existential despair behind a dapper façade. To the shocked surprise of the literary emigration, he committed suicide.

9
The Literary Scene

Stefan Zweig was but one of many exiles who escaped from the personal and professional hardship of existence in death. Suicide was quite common among the rank and file of the literary emigrants, and heart failure assumed almost epidemic proportions. But the vast majority of the exile authors continued their struggle to live and work against overwhelming odds. The most traumatic and crippling difficulty they encountered as writers was the near impossibility of getting their works printed. Hardly any of them were well enough known in the United States for American publishers to be interested in bringing out their writings in translation. The numerous publishing enterprises set up by the emigrants themselves devoted only part of their production to exile literature. Although the supply of books from Switzerland was not seriously interrupted during the war, the demand for reprints of the classics and other standard works could not be met with imports alone. Enterprising exiles therefore entered the publishing field for the specific purpose of supplying these works as well as German translations of fiction from other languages.

Against all these odds there was still a steady output of literary texts by exile writers. Between 1933 and 1947 well over a hundred titles were printed in the United States. The size of the editions ranged from extremely few copies to a very respectable ten thousand. The scope of the publishing enterprises themselves was no less varied. There were one-man operations that produced no more than a single title and large-scale undertakings that engaged in a variety of publishing ventures. Sometimes they even competed with well-established American firms in the field of English translations of German works. With few exceptions, however, the sale of their German texts was very limited. Apart from the language barrier, the lack of distribution and publicity facilities was a major marketing problem. But in any case, the generally disinterested or even hostile attitude on the part of the German-Americans and the fact that more often than not the exiles themselves simply could not afford to buy books severely reduced the potential market for German-language works.

The various aspects of exile publishing were all reflected in the activities of Gottfried Bermann Fischer, who was the first of the major German publishers to establish himself in America. His enterprise in Sweden kept going throughout the war years as one of the most significant producers of antifascist literature. Bermann Fischer himself came to New York at the end of June 1940. He did not consider German-language publishing to be economically feasible in the United States. With the support of the American book industry he therefore in the following year launched the English-language house L. B. Fischer Publishing Company. His partner in this enterprise was F. H. Landshoff, a veteran of exile publishing in Holland.

The firm made available numerous translations of German works, including texts by exile writers, such as Klaus Mann's autobiography *The Turning Point* (*Der Wendepunkt*). Some of these books were translated directly from the manuscript and appeared in their original form only much later, if at all. Only two German-language projects were undertaken by the American branch of Fischer. One consisted of small reprint editions for the local market of some few best-selling titles by Thomas Mann and Franz Werfel. The other was a cheap paperback series of popular fiction both exile and pre-exile. Furthermore the firm produced small mimeographed or photomechanically reproduced token editions of some works by Mann and Werfel in order to protect the American copyright on them.

Apart from this the publication of German texts was left to the Stockholm firm. These books were, as far as circumstances allowed, imported from Sweden and distributed in the States through regular trade channels. Under Bermann Fischer's remote control the Stockholm house issued almost fifty exile literature titles, including the major novels written in America by Thomas Mann and Franz Werfel. The extremely difficult mail connection between Sweden and the United States made it usually impossible for the American-based authors to proofread their books themselves. As a result the editions concerned are highly unreliable textually and full of printing errors. The actual manufacturing of some of these works was carried out in Switzerland. In that case, because of a trade agreement between Sweden and Germany, the printed sheets of these anti-Nazi exile books were openly transported by rail through the Third Reich!

Other experienced publishers in exile shared Bermann Fischer's dim view on the viability of German-language books in the United States. Kurt Wolff played a leading role in Germany in the twenties with the publication of numerous books by the best-known avant-garde and expressionist writers. He reestablished himself in New York when he arrived there in 1941, and his Pantheon Books soon gained him considerable prestige as an internationally oriented publisher. Wolff made his most significant contribution to exile literature with the publication of Hermann Broch's major opus *The Death of Vergil*, which appeared in 1945. Otherwise he included scarcely any German titles in his program.

Considering the circumstances under which it operated, the exile publishing industry developed a level of activity that was little short of amazing, and occasionally it even came up with an international best-seller. Even so, it was impossible for all except a very few writers to make a living with their pens. The problem was further compounded by the state of the exile daily and periodical press. Traditionally most of the writers had depended for a considerable part of their earnings on newspapers and journals to which they contributed comments, essays, fiction, poetry, and reviews. Many writers had also held editorial posts, but in exile these opportunities were drastically reduced. Although in America as in other host countries innumerable exile publications existed, almost all of them were so small and lacking in resources that they could pay only nominal fees and salaries, if any.

Only those few exile-oriented papers that had their origins in existing, established organs tended to be better endowed. Their relative affluence could of course benefit only a very small number of the emigrant writers. One of these publications was the *Neue Volks-Zeitung*, which with some exaggeration has been called the only genuine German emigrant newspaper in the whole of the United States. Since the 1870's the *New Yorker Volkszeitung* had been the mouthpiece of the German-American socialist movement. Over the years the steadily progressing assimilation of the immigrant group concerned deprived the paper of much of its readership. The general decline of the socialist cause in American public life even further reduced its viability, and in October 1932 it was forced to cease publication.

Two months later it was revived under the name *Neue Volks-Zeitung*, edited and written predominantly by skilled and experienced journalists from Germany. In its new guise the paper continued to cater to what was left of its traditional reading public. At the same time it sought to appeal to the new refugees who were beginning to come into the country in ever-increasing numbers. Basically it still hewed to a conservatively socialist political line that was consistent with the ideological orientation of the German-American labor organizations, but gradually the tone changed. The old guard readers objected to the allegedly typical German arrogance of the new people in charge as much as to the paper's changing focus. Over their protests the *Neue Volks-Zeitung* devoted itself more and more to the interests of a certain segment of the exile community. It came to be so closely linked to the rather doctrinaire German Social Democratic party in exile that it did not represent the views of the increasingly conservatively inclined majority of the emigrants.

The ideological bias of the *Neue Volks-Zeitung* probably helped make *Der Aufbau* the most prestigious and influential organ of the antifascist exile. So far as its origin was concerned, this publication certainly was not predestined to play this role. It had come into existence as a stenciled information sheet, distributed free of charge to the members of the New World Club in New York. That association had been founded in 1924 by German-Jewish immigrants. With the influx of European Jews in the late twenties and especially after 1933, the membership of the club increased very rapidly. By 1937 it had become so large that the original format of *Der Aufbau* was not adequate anymore. To keep up with the changing times, the journal needed a professional editor.

The first to be appointed to this post was Rudolf Brandl, who held the office for only a year before he was forced to resign over a dispute between established immigrants and anti-Nazi exiles. This clash was typical of many confrontations between new arrivals and long-time residents. Jealousy and conflicts of interest and opinion between the two groups were the order of the day. In this particular instance the recent arrivals gained the upper hand and appointed one of their own, former Berlin newspaperman Manfred George, to the editorship. George drastically changed the entire nature of the publication. From an occasional club sheet it was turned into a regular weekly. Instead of being distributed free, *Der Aufbau* from this time on was sold by subscription and on the newsstands, and to the general public as well as to the membership of the New World Club.

The subsequent development of *Der Aufbau* was a journalistic success story. The circulation which in 1930 had been around 3,000 ten years later had reached the 13,000 mark. By 1942 this figure had doubled and after another two years *Der Aufbau* sold some 30,500 copies. It was read not only in the United States but also in Palestine and throughout the world. The American government regarded it as the authoritative voice of German antifascism. Nevertheless *Der Aufbau* basically always remained a journal serving the interests of those German-speaking Jews who were immigrants in the true sense of the word. It spoke to and for those people who intended to settle permanently in the United States, integrate with American society, and forget about their country of origin. The journal's basic outlook therefore differed greatly from the attitude of the exile writers whose only real interest lay in Hitler's eventual downfall and their own return to Europe. This difference in orientation sharply limited the importance of *Der Aufbau* as an outlet for the exile writers' work and as a source of income for them.

The virtual impossibility of making even a minimal income in their own trade condemned most exile writers to material hardship, if not downright penury. Even Thomas Mann, who was generally assumed to be living in the lap of luxury during his American exile, in reality had only a very modest income. During the last war years, for instance, he got five hundred dollars per month from his American publisher Alfred Knopf. In addition he received the same amount from Mrs. Eugene Meyer, wife of the *Washington Post* publisher, in the guise of a salary for his token appointment as "Advisor to the Library of Congress for Germanic Languages." Others less well known than he were generally much worse off and were often reduced to performing routine clerical or menial jobs for which they were usually physically as well as mentally utterly unsuited.

Many exile writers were at times forced to live on charity and handouts of one kind or another. Prominent novelist Alfred Döblin early in 1942 wrote to a friend that he and his family existed on eighteen dollars unemployment benefits plus twenty dollars from a private charitable organization. Shortly before that Döblin had actually been relatively well off as one of the beneficiaries of a scheme initiated, possibly with the encouragement of the government, by the film industry.

During the early part of the century Germany had been an extremely important center of the budding film industry. German filmmakers had given the cinematographic art decisive impulses with such classic silent movies as *The Cabinet of Dr. Caligari* and *The Last Laugh.* In the late twenties the impact of technical developments like the sound film and the economic chaos of the Great Depression had caused the German film to lose its leading position. As a consequence many of the top producers, directors, and actors moved to the United States, among them Ernst Lubitsch, Pola Negri, F. W. Murnau, and Conrad Veidt.

By the time the literary refugees from Nazism began to flock to the United States, a number of these pioneers had risen to positions of power and wealth in the Hollywood film world. It was partly owing to their influence that quite a few of the exile authors were offered one-year contracts as script writers at a rate of a hundred dollars per week by Warner Brothers and Metro Goldwyn Mayer. These appointments enabled the new arrivals to find their feet in the new country and solved their most immediate financial problems.

While the benefits of the arrangement were duly appreciated by the emigrants, they also felt humiliated and frustrated by it. Their professional pride was wounded by the fact that the regular American script writers, whom they regarded as their artistic inferiors, earned substantially higher salaries. Even more disturbing was the creative futility to which their appointments condemned them. A private office and a secretary were made available to them, and they were supposed to put in regular nine-to-five working days. But they were seldom given anything to do, and if they did receive an assignment it almost always concerned a project that the studio had no intention of realizing anyway. At the same time the uncongenial environment and atmosphere prevented most of them from using their office hours to pursue their own literary work.

Occasionally a writer from whom on the basis of his status in the European world of letters the film people expected to get usable scripts was given much more favorable conditions. Carl Zuckmayer with a number of highly successful stage plays and films had become one of the most popular European authors of the period between the wars. Upon his arrival in Hollywood he received a seven-year contract at a starting salary of seven hundred and fifty dollars per month. Even this did not for long reconcile him with the spirit prevailing in the studio.

The film adaptation of Arnold Zweig's novel *The Fight over Sergeant Grischka* (*Der Streit um den Sergeanten Grischka*), on which Zuckmayer worked at first, had been a worthwhile and challenging project. But suddenly he was ordered to drop this script and instead write a melodramatic Don Juan movie intended as a vehicle for Errol Flynn. He refused the assignment, knowing that this would mean his dismissal from a lucrative job. Zuckmayer then went to New York where for a brief period he joined the staff of the New School for Social Research. He was employed as a lecturer in the Dramatic Workshop led by exiled epic theater director Erwin Piscator. The pay was very low and after a while Zuckmayer resigned from his teaching position. He leased a property in the mountains of Vermont, where he spent the rest of his exile making an austere but dignified living as a farmer. Such resourcefulness and energy were very rare among the exiles.

Alfred Döblin also at one point was engaged on a rather more meaningful script writing assignment, only to find himself suddenly in disfavor with his employers. He was asked to give an opinion on the sentimental subject matter of *Mrs. Miniver*, which was being considered for a film idealizing the English nation. Döblin lost his credibility when he suggested that the story would provide a good vehicle for Charlie Chaplin.

One of the very few script writing exiles ever to see one of his works filmed was Bertolt Brecht. In the summer of 1941 he reached California by way of the Russian port of Vladivostok. He settled in Santa Monica where he soon surrounded himself again with a tight clique of collaborators and hangers-on from the burgeoning exile colony there. Brecht furthermore was one of the few exile authors who because of his reputation and life style numbered some prominent local personalities among his acquaintances, including W. H. Auden, Aldous Huxley, Charles Chaplin, and Charles Laughton. He also knew personally a number of the established film people who originally hailed from Germany. Moreover he had always been interested in the film medium and had before his exile occupied himself with it both theoretically and practically.

Owing to his connections and his expertise, Brecht's script writing career in Hollywood did bear some fruit. In 1943 United Artists made the movie *Hangmen Also Die* directed by the well-known emigrated German director Fritz Lang. It dealt with Heydrich, the Gestapo chief and highest Nazi administrator in occupied Czechoslovakia, who was killed by partisans.

In spite of his relatively favorable experiences with the American film industry, Brecht's views on it were bitterly critical. In a satirical poem entitled "Hollywood" he accused it of insincerity and noted the corrupting influence of the prevailing atmosphere.

The opportunistic climate of the movie business could hardly have come as a surprise to Brecht. In the twenties in Germany he had indulged in lengthy legal proceedings against the filmmakers who according to him had perverted his original *Three Penny Opera* for the sake of profit. In spite of this experience, economic necessity forced him to subject himself to the allegedly demeaning conditions prevailing in the Hollywood establishment. He was no more successful than most other exiles in transplanting his literary career to the United States. Except for some contributions to various exile journals, scarcely anything of his was published in America during the war years. In order to maintain at least some contact with a small circle of readers within the exile community, he was even forced to distribute stenciled copies of some of his new poetry. Productions of his plays were limited to a few German language performances by emigrant actors, although in 1943 two of his major pieces were premiered in Zurich, Switzerland.

Undaunted by the lack of publishing and performance opportunities in his country of exile, Bertolt Brecht remained very active throughout his American sojourn. The works he created in close collaboration with friends and disciples, as was his custom, represent a qualitative high point of his career and transcend all dogmatic party lines. They include his play about the Italian renaissance scholar Galileo Galilei, who under pressure of the Roman Catholic church retracted his heretical discovery that the earth revolved around the sun but secretly continued his work. The title figure was conceived as a role for Charles Laughton, who later did appear in an English version. Brecht worked together with the actor on the play in spite of the fact that he spoke little English and Laughton knew no German.[1]

The work dealt with the theme of the scientist's ethical responsibility, which through the development of nuclear physics and its military applications had become particularly topical. But even more stress was placed on Galileo's basically unprincipled opportunism and on his egocentric nature, symbolized in his gluttony. The view that the end of survival justifies any means also provided the central motif of a work that Brecht undertook in the early years of his American exile. His play *Schweyk in the Second World War* (*Schweyk im zweiten Weltkrieg*) was an adaptation of a novel by the Czech author Jaroslav Hašek, which depicted how the simpleton Schweyk by virtue of his total lack of integrity had managed to survive the First World War.

The idea was most congenial to Brecht, and not only in the

realm of literary abstractions. Throughout his life he practiced the art of compromise, be it with truth or with principles, in order to protect his personal interests. A notable occasion was his appearance before the House Un-American Activities Committee on 30 October 1947. HUAC at this time, like Senator Joseph McCarthy's group, focused its attention on Hollywood, which harbored many people of known or suspected leftist orientation. Brecht was small fry and personally not of much interest to the committee, which was mainly concerned with obtaining from him evidence about other, more illustrious suspects.

Previous witnesses from among Brecht's acquaintances had already been questioned about his associations with particular people and organizations and about the opinions he held. The panel that interrogated him was chaired by Representative J. Parnell Thomas, and one of its three members was Richard M. Nixon. The committee's investigator Robert E. Stripling did most of the actual questioning. Brecht was assisted by two lawyers with extensive experience in such hearings, and a translator.

The proceedings started with the formal identification of Brecht. His name, birthplace, birth date, and his various countries of exile before his arrival in the United States were entered into the record. At this point he unsuccessfully sought permission to read a carefully prepared statement that he had brought with him. Then the questioning turned to Brecht's occupation, which he described as playwright and poet. This led to a discussion of his connection with the Hollywood movie industry, and mention was made of the script for the film *Hangmen Also Die.*

The interrogation next focused on Brecht's relationship with the Marxist composer Hanns Eisler, who had provided music for several of his stage works. The question was also raised whether Brecht himself was or ever had been a member of the Communist Party. Brecht again requested permission to read his statement. He was directed to submit it to the chairman who looked through it and remarked that it was "a very interesting story of German life" but not at all relevant to the inquiry. He denied Brecht permission to present it to the committee, and the questioning about his relationship with the Communist Party continued. After hinting that he deemed the inquiry to be legally improper but as a guest in the United States did not want to argue the issue, Brecht categorically denied ever having been a Party member.

Mr. Stripling next turned to the topic of Brecht's literary production, which he criticized as being "very revolutionary." Brecht parried the remark by associating that aspect of his writings with his opposition against the Hitler regime, but the committee was totally uninterested in his observations. The investigator then brought up a very recent contribution of Brecht in an East German publication as evidence of the playwright's Marxist outlook. Brecht managed to defuse this damaging point at least to some extent, observing that the text in question was not a new article but a scene from a play written some ten years earlier.

Mr. Stripling next introduced a topic that could not so easily be disposed of. In dealing with it Brecht was forced to evade and distort the truth considerably. At stake was his play *The Measure Taken* (*Die Maßnahme*). It is undeniably one of his most doctrinaire Communist works, in which he expounds on the idea that the individual must sacrifice his very life if Party discipline demands it. At first Brecht tried to confuse the issue by saying that the work was based on an ancient Japanese No play that dealt with the subject of religious idealism. The committee spokesman was not that easily fooled and forced the evasive playwright to admit that the piece did indeed have to do with Communism. Brecht tried to escape into generalizations about the right and duty of literature to represent the ideas of its time. He also linked *The Measure Taken* with the German workers' fight against Hitler.

Mr. Stripling then read a brief excerpt from the text, culminating in the main character's death at the hands of his fellow Party members. The text established beyond any doubt that the play was a piece of blatant Marxist propaganda. With considerable irony the committee chairman summed up Brecht's shifty prevarications with the observation that the victim in the play "was just killed, he was not murdered." And so the hearing went on about Brecht's visits to Moscow, about interviews in which he had espoused the Marxist cause, and about the accuracy of the

English versions of some of his political poetry. Brecht pleaded ignorance, protested his innocence, and accused his translators of grossly distorting his work.

His explanations and assertions were anything but convincing, but the committee had by now lost all interest in him. Even his most transparent self-contradictions were scarcely challenged any longer. Finally the chairman dismissed him with a rather sarcastic compliment about his exemplary and cooperative attitude. On the following day Brecht left the United States by plane for Switzerland. From there he went to East Germany, where until his death in 1956 he faithfully served the Communist dictatorship as cultural figurehead and director of his own state-supported theater in Berlin.

It has become customary to speak with awe and admiration of Brecht's cunning on the occasion of the HUAC hearing. In the view of most commentators only the stupidity and lack of preparation of his interrogators limited the dramatist's achievement in outwitting them. The transcript of the hearing does not quite bear out this opinion. Instead it conveys the impression of an investigator who knew perfectly well where the truth lay. He obviously derived some satisfaction from seeing Brecht squirm under his questions and incriminating quotations but simply could not be bothered to press the matter. Bertolt Brecht was always intent on promoting a very flattering public image of himself. With the aid of fawning literary historians he carefully nurtured the myth of his resounding victory over the dumb Washington bureaucrats. In reality this final episode of his American sojourn was typical and symptomatic of the exile writers' ineffectiveness in their confrontations with those who wielded real power.

In keeping with his tendency to sail with the prevailing winds and to rate survival above principle, Brecht took care not to become involved in exile politics during his stay in America. Thomas Mann was not quite so cautious and burned his fingers on several political schemes and conflicts before settling on a middle-of-the-road position. But even though he learned the hard way to avoid close association with any political group or cause, he kept getting embroiled in controversies. Ever since the twenties he had made it a habit to speak his mind freely and publicly on the dangers of fascist totalitarianism. The effectiveness and resonance of his letters to Eduard Korrodi and the dean of Bonn University in 1936 had irrevocably cast him in the role of a political figure.

Still in the same year Mann gave a talk in Budapest using a writers' conference as his forum. At the time Hungary was already very much in the shadow of the rising Nazi menace across the border, and the government was doing all it could to avoid anything that might be regarded as a provocation of its powerful neighbor. The conference was intended to be purely literary and avoid all political polemics. Thomas Mann at one point during the proceedings suddenly took the floor and delivered a fiery impromptu speech in which he bitterly denounced the "assassins of freedom" and proclaimed the urgency of bringing into being a militant democracy. How much importance was attached to his words becomes clear from the fact that the Nazis themselves alluded to this incident when they revoked the novelist's citizenship. The proclamation specifically cited his participation in demonstrations of "international associations, usually under Jewish influence, whose hostile attitude toward Germany was generally known."

Thomas Mann became increasingly active and involved politically. He devoted his fourth visit to the United States in 1938 largely to the propagation of his anti-Nazi views. During this trip he gave his talk on "The Coming Victory of Democracy" in fifteen cities throughout the country. It made him widely known among the American public as one of the foremost champions of the opposition against the Hitler regime. The fact that during his lecture tour the Anschluß of Austria took place made his message all the more topical and effective. While delivering this talk in Los Angeles, Thomas Mann broadly hinted that he regarded his exile as at least semipermanent. He also indicated that he planned to spend it in the United States.

The formulation he used on this occasion—"where I am, there is Germany,"—was hardly modest, but the self-assurance it expressed boosted the spirits of the exile community considerably. In one sense Mann's statement was scarcely an exaggeration because he had indeed by this time become the unchallenged leader and spokesman of the emigration. His authority in this respect was acknowledged even by those exiles who opposed his views and specific actions. The public and the authorities in America and other host countries also regarded him as the key figure among the antifascist refugees. His status was confirmed by the professorship that Princeton bestowed on him in the fall of 1938, at the beginning of Thomas Mann's fifteen-year stay in the United States.

Soon he made contact and developed personal relations with numerous highly placed people in public and political life, including President Roosevelt and the publisher of the *Washington Post*, Eugene Meyer, who in time became a very close friend of his. But Mann's established position as a public figure did not shield him from the pitfalls of political intrigue and infighting among the emigrants. Mann had for instance allowed himself to be named as president of the European section of the American Guild for German Cultural Freedom. The Guild had been founded in 1936 by the conservative aristocrat Hubertus Friedrich, Prince of Löwenstein. It seemed a reputable organization that could be of much use to the emigrant writers, but Mann soon had reason to regret that he had become involved in it. In October 1937 the Guild held a competition for the best book manuscript written by an exile author. The publicity and response were overwhelming, and 170 texts were submitted. Unfortunately no award could be made because it appeared that the organizers had helped themselves to the prize money. Although Thomas Mann at this point hastily backed out, the scandal inevitably embarrassed and hurt him.

The experience made him more careful about political schemes. But as it turned out he still was not cautious enough and let himself be drawn into the so-called Free Germany Movement, which aimed at the formation of a German shadow government in exile that could take over the reins in Germany as soon as the Nazis were defeated. Thomas Mann prudently rejected all proposals that he should occupy a prominent position in this project. In the end the novelist was prevailed upon to use his personal connections to sound out high administration circles. Mann traveled to the nation's capital, where the issue met with a uniformly negative reaction on the part of Washington officials. While the re-buttal must have been personally unpleasant to Mann, he was politically relieved by it, for the whole notion of a government in exile ran directly counter to his own philosophy. His ambiguous approach to the matter aroused the ire of the Free Germany Movement, and so Mann ended by being caught in the middle.

Even the best of intentions were no adequate safeguard against such debacles, as Thomas Mann found out in connection with the Council for a Democratic Germany. This body, in which he and theologian Paul Tillich played the leading roles, was constituted to represent the interests of all emigrants. In keeping with this aim and with Mann's personal views, the Council was intent on transcending the various party lines. All ideological directions within the exile community were to be included. It was precisely this impartiality that got Thomas Mann in hot water on this occasion. Many feared that it would enable the Communists to take over the organization and use it for their own purposes.

This concern was not too farfetched. The experiences of other groups had amply demonstrated the dangers of such an ecumeni-cal attitude. The German-American Cultural League (Deutsch-amerikanischer Kulturverband) was a case in point. It had been brought under Communist leadership after all the representatives of other political convictions had gradually been maneuvered out of their influential posts. The same fate had befallen the German American Writers Association. Under the chairmanship of Oskar Maria Graf it had identified so unreservedly with the Russian dictator that it was called an "agency of Stalin." In 1939 many members resigned out of protest against the German-Russian nonaggression pact. Thomas Mann had been honorary president both of the Cultural League and of the Writers Association. He hastily resigned from both of these organizations when the Com-munist Party took control of them. Early in 1942 they merged to form the German-American Emergency Conference. Mann hence-forth sided with its rival body the German American Congress for Democracy.

His unhappy experiences made Thomas Mann steer a middle course. He refused to become vice-president of the League of American Writers on the grounds that it was Communist oriented or at least unduly influenced by left-wing elements. He also steadfastly refused to join in the anti-Communist agitation that took on ever more fanatical form as the war and the military partnership with Russia approached an end. On the whole Mann's well-meaning political actions and gestures in his American exile misfired badly. Trying to reconcile differences and unite factions, he actually tended to add fuel to the strife between the different exile groups. In the end his unlucky touch even made him lose some of his influence and prestige in emigration circles.

The disappointments and frustrations that resulted from his attempts at direct political action undoubtedly strengthened Thomas Mann's natural tendency to rely mainly on the power of the literary word. He expressed his convictions and developed his views especially clearly in his Moses novella *The Law* (*Das Gesetz*). Another important work in this connection was the epic tetralogy *Joseph and His Brothers* (*Joseph und seine Brüder*) in which the exile experience was artistically sublimated. But his greatest novel was *Dr. Faustus* (*Doktor Faustus*), the voluminous story of an avant-garde composer whose cold genius, ultimate insanity, and death symbolized the greatness and fall of the German nation. On the clinical level Faustus's demonic creativity, collapse, and death were due to syphilis. The disease represented the German people's infection with fascism. This motif further linked the main character to the nineteenth-century philosopher Friedrich Nietzsche, some of whose views had been adopted by the Nazis.

At the same time the composer's rise and fall were attributed to a pact with the devil. Through this theme the title figure is associated with his historical and literary ancestor. The life of sixteenth-century scholar-magician Faust has over the ages inspired many authors, including Marlowe and Goethe. In Goethe's treatment Faust had become the classical embodiment of German idealism. In this way Thomas Mann indirectly connected Germany's philosophical heritage with the spirit of fascism. But in spite of these negative implications, the novel also reflects the aging writer's nostalgic yearning for his native soil.

Dr. Faustus was to a large extent an attempt to conjure up Germany's real essence in figures and scenes of a somewhat idealized past. This aspect of *Dr. Faustus* was echoed in the works of other exile writers, some of whom likewise used the Faust motif. Leonhard Frank's *German Novella* (*Deutsche Novelle*), for instance, corresponded so closely to *Dr. Faustus* in theme and conception that Thomas Mann hinted at plagiarism. Mann himself was in turn accused by Arnold Schoenberg of having made illegitimate use of that composer's intellectual property, for the technique of composition attributed to Faustus in Mann's novel greatly resembles the twelve-tone system.

While Mann divided his time between his public, political, and literary concerns, Franz Werfel in his American exile devoted himself entirely to his writing. He wrote several books that met with wide popular acclaim and allowed him to live in the rather grand style to which he was accustomed. The first of his works that established his fame and fortune in America, *The Song of Bernadette* (*Das Lied der Bernadette*), was thematically connected with his flight from Europe to the United States. He had delayed his departure from France until it was almost too late and did not leave Paris until several days after German troops had occupied the city.

Traveling by car and train he finally reached Bordeaux, where the only shelter he could find was in a brothel that had temporarily suspended its normal activities in order to cash in on the presence of thousands of refugees from the north. From there Werfel went on to Biarritz where he hoped to get the necessary papers and visas to continue his journey. When he failed to obtain the travel documents he moved on to Lourdes to recuperate from the strain and hardships of his flight. He stayed in this well-known place of pilgrimage for several weeks. During this time he immersed himself in the history and legend of the alleged appearances of the Virgin Mary to the half-witted peasant girl Bernadette Soubirous in the year 1858.

Meanwhile it became obvious that Werfel would not be able to obtain the needed permits for crossing the border into Spain. This left him no choice but to escape illegally from the ever more hostile and dangerous realm of the fascist puppet regime in Vichy. This always highly dangerous undertaking was in his case made even more perilous by his physical condition, for a long history of heart trouble had culminated a short time before this in his first serious coronary attack. Under these circumstances Werfel on the last day of his stay in Lourdes made a vow that he would write a novel about the Bernadette miracle if he succeeded in making his way to the United States.

He reached New York in the middle of October 1940 and by the end of the year arrived in Los Angeles. He moved into a luxurious house whose personnel reportedly included a butler. Two months later in fulfillment of his vow he began to write *The Song of Bernadette*. Toward the end of 1941 the original German version appeared in Stockholm, and early in the following year an English translation was published in America. It became tremendously popular and was the Book of the Month Club selection for May 1942. Werfel sold the film rights for $100,000. The movie, starring Jenifer Jones in her first big role, was released just before Christmas 1943 and won five Academy Awards. The advertising campaign for the film somewhat blatantly exploited the background story of Werfel's vow, though Werfel himself had mentioned the incident only briefly in the preface to the novel. In the work itself there were no references or allusions to current world events. It was a predominantly factual, only moderately stylized, documentary account of the alleged miracle.

If *The Song of Bernadette* was an apolitical work it had pronounced religious connotations. The choice of topic and its treatment clearly reflected Werfel's preoccupation with Roman Catholicism. It appealed to him not only on religious grounds but also and perhaps primarily because its pomp and ritual struck a responsive chord in his essentially operatic heart. Even so, he never formally converted because he regarded Israel as an essential concrete witness to the Revelation. Without it Christianity would be reduced to the level of a shadowy mythology. Werfel moreover did not want to desert the ranks of the Jews in their darkest hour of persecution and genocide by the fascists. According to him their anti-Semitism was only superficially racist in nature. In his opinion it was basically a form of metaphysical enmity against Christ and the Christian doctrines that aim at overcoming man's fallen state.

In contrast to *The Song of Bernadette*, Werfel's next work dealt directly with contemporary events. *Jacobowsky and the Colonel*

(*Jacobowsky und der Oberst*) was a play about the desperate flight of the antifascist refugees before the advancing German army through France in the summer of 1940. This work like the preceding one had its roots in Werfel's stay in Lourdes. He occupied a hotel room next to the Polish banker S. S. Jacobowitz, who was also trying to flee the country. Jacobowitz told Werfel about his various adventures, which form the basis of the play. Later, much to Werfel's disgust, Jacobowitz claimed a percentage of the royalties for having provided the plot, even though his story had actually in the dramatization been supplemented with some of the writer's personal experiences. Like the main character, Werfel had to escape the approaching Nazi forces on no fewer than five successive occasions. His adventures with the car he rented for eight thousand francs to take him from Paris to Carcassonne also went into this "comedy of a tragedy," and so did the equally exorbitant taxi ride from Bordeaux to Biarritz that cost him six thousand francs.

Jacobowsky and the Colonel wavers stylistically between tragedy and broad farce, between the obvious and the grotesque, between stark realism and dreamlike vision. The play deals with the flight of the Jew Jacobowsky and the arrogant anti-Semitic Polish colonel. Intending to escape to southern France ahead of the advancing German forces, they are traveling together in Jacobowsky's car, which is driven by the colonel's servant. But once under way the colonel instructs his man to drive north. Jacobowsky's horrified protests are ignored as regardless of their life and safety they penetrate ever deeper into the battle zone.

It then becomes clear that the colonel is defying the approaching German army for the sake of a love affair. He is willing to sacrifice everybody and everything to keep a proto-absurd rendezvous behind the German lines. Against a background of artillery bombardments the colonel stages a violin and mouth organ serenade under the balcony of his beloved. She appears and claims to have been executed fifteen minutes earlier by German soldiers who were dressed half in uniform and half in animal skins.

One of the more impressive scenes in the play depicts a crowd of emigrants in a café in Marseilles. The police burst in to raid the place and the refugees flee in panic. Only one of them remains, sitting at his table behind an empty glass. Unable to bear the tensions and uncertainties of his existence any longer, he has taken poison. In complete contrast to this moving episode, at another point the Wandering Jew and St. Francis appear on a tandem bicycle.

Elsewhere a surrealistic element interrupts the action with a figure who is identified only as "the tragic gentleman." His appearance is accompanied by the sound of footsteps of the thousands of Parisians who are fleeing before the German troops. As he launches into a reflective soliloquy the shuffling and tramping noises change into a rhythmic musical framework for his words. While he speaks people come streaming out of the hotel, weighted down with luggage, and disappear off stage whispering among themselves. The entire scene should according to Franz Werfel's stage directions resemble a mysterious ballet.

Sudden alternation of realism and surrealism was almost a structural characteristic of this kind of exile writing, occurring in quite a number of works. The narrative stance in Bernard von Bretano's novel *Trial without a Judge* (*Prozeß ohne Richter*), a rather cautious story published in 1937 about Nazi intimidation and terror tactics, vacillates between these perspectives. Anna Segher's 1944 novel, *Transit*, dealing with a refugee in Marseilles who under the name of a dead man tries to obtain a visa, shows a similar stylistic dualism.

The main character in Segher's novel remarks that exile life seemed "like one of those parts of reality that are mixed up with dreams." These words accurately describe the expressive nature of the exile texts concerned. The extreme example of *Jakobowsky* indicates that the contemporary literary reflections of refugee life at times leave all actual impressions far behind in absurdist flights of fancy. The impact of the exile experience on the writer's mind may in part be responsible for this tendency. The private sensations on which such writings were based had been extremely traumatic. The authors' personal feelings were so deeply involved that they were incapable of mentally standing back from their subject matter in order to impose a consistent artistic form on it.

So vivid and painful were their memories that the realism of the scenes they described overwhelmed their powers of literary composition. The thematic substance resisted artistic sublimation through the creative imagination. The interspersed surrealistic elements represent a desperate attempt, conscious or unconscious, to compensate for the lack of uniform stylization. In the absurd scenes the creative leavening that could not be integrated into the realistic body of the work is, as it were, lumped together. The net result is one of incoherence and disintegration. The authors were very conscious of this problem. Werfel for instance rewrote *Jacobowsky and the Colonel* innumerable times and even then remained unsatisfied with the play.

Jacobowsky and the Colonel was first performed in New York in March 1944 in an English translation by Sam N. Behrmann. Werfel disapproved of the adaptation, claiming that it distorted his work, and undoubtedly there was some loss of subtlety and complexity. Still it is evident that the changes made in the English version also corrected the fundamental weaknesses in the original text. Once Werfel's all too close personal, emotional involvement in the subject matter had been remedied, the material proved very effective. In the more objective form of the Broadway adaptation, *Jacobowsky and the Colonel* escaped the fate of almost all exile literature of falling on deaf ears. It proved overwhelmingly successful with the general American public, and a later film version starring Danny Kaye was also a box office hit.

Meanwhile, the condition of Werfel's heart had continued to deteriorate, until toward the end of 1942 he had suffered such a massive seizure that the physicians gave up all hope. Even so he recovered again to some degree, only to be struck down less than a year later with another series of heart attacks. Afterward Werfel's extremely serious and weak condition forced him to live with his personal physician in a bungalow in Santa Barbara. By now he was working on his last book, the big futuristic novel *Star of the Unborn (Stern der Ungeborenen)*. In this artistically and philosophically daring work he incorporated his own intimate acquaintance with death.

It is a "travel novel" set in a time aeons away in which the main character, who is designated as "F. W.," is resurrected. The topic did not offer obvious opportunities for politically salient comments. Only in the case of the idol "Hiltier" was there a direct and explicit reference to the German dictator. His name was at first even given as "Heiltier" and he was saluted by the people with the greeting "Heil Hiltier." In the ironical tone that pervades the book there was moreover a distinct element of criticism aimed at the ever increasing collectivization of life.

In the middle of August 1945 the manuscript of the novel was complete and a week later Franz Werfel died. He was buried in his dinner suit like the protagonist of *Star of the Unborn*. But unlike his literary alter ego who after his resurrection complained that he did not have a clean handkerchief and could not see clearly because he had been interred without his glasses, the writer was laid to rest equipped with both.

10
Victory?

When Franz Werfel died the war in Europe had been over for some three months. But the Allied victory in May 1945 elicited very mixed feelings on the part of the emigrants. With the sharpened political sensitivity of the persecuted and dispossessed they were as a group acutely aware of the shortcomings of the postwar world. They were particularly conscious of the increasingly tense relations between the Western democracies and Russia. Within the United States the disenchantment with the wartime ally manifested itself in a rising tide of feeling that it would have been better to make common cause with the fascists against the Communist bloc. The ever more widespread, rabid anti-Communism was deeply disturbing to most of the exile authors with their liberal or leftist sympathies. It seemed to give the lie to the proposition to which they had devoted their lives, that fascism was the greatest danger Western civilization had ever confronted. The general upsurge of anti-Marxist sentiments therefore in the minds of many of these writers overshadowed the military defeat of Germany and the downfall of the Hitler regime. It added to the sense of isolation and frustration that the years of emigration had instilled in them.

While the political mood of the country gave the exiles cause for concern that the people had after all failed to recognize fascism as the archenemy of democracy and civilization, most of the emigrant authors thought that the Allies were too harsh in their attitude toward the defeated foe. In their opinion the insistence on an unconditional surrender by Germany failed to take into account the difference between the hard-core Nazis and the rank and file of the German people. Many of the exiles had experienced the rise of fascism at first hand, and they knew only too well how the harsh conditions imposed on Germany after World War I in the Treaty of Versailles had been exploited by Hitler. Based on this experience they thought that the unbending attitude of the victors contained the seeds of future conflict and turmoil. These and other circumstances such as the expected difficulties in changing over from a war to a peacetime economy caused a general sense of foreboding. In the minds of most exiles such apprehensive feelings crystallized in the death of President Roosevelt on 12 April 1945, when the final military victory over Germany was only a few weeks away.

Some exiles had at first had reservations about Roosevelt. In spite of these initial doubts the great majority of them, exemplified by Thomas Mann, soon developed an esteem for him that bordered on hero worship. Mann paid him high tribute by endowing the title figure of his great tetralogy *Joseph and his Brothers* with some of the president's personality traits. On one occasion when he was a guest at the White House, the novelist was struck by "the Hermes-like nature of the man." The decisive factor in the exile authors' admiration for Roosevelt was his achievement in bringing America into the war against strong isolationist currents within the country. For this development, which assured the ultimate defeat of Hitler Germany, Mann later gave the president sole credit.

The literary emigration regarded Roosevelt as a statesman of the highest order. In their opinion he was the only one among the Allied leaders who could have solved the tremendous political problems that inevitably would erupt with the end of the armed conflict. So strongly did many of the exiles believe in Roosevelt as the only potential savior of the world that his death on the eve of Germany's capitulation filled them with despair. They felt that without him all their own efforts and sacrifices for the sake of a better future had been in vain.

Even aside from their fears and doubts about the shape of political things to come, the exiles were not able to rejoice wholeheartedly in the defeat of the regime that had brought them so much suffering. The general public had known of the massive Allied bombardments on the cities of Germany for some time, but only after the end of the war, as the first eyewitness reports came in, was the extent of the devastation and destruction fully realized. Large parts of the country were so ravaged that all emigrants whose relatives or friends had spent the war years in Germany had reason to fear the worst. And even for those who had survived the holocaust of battle and bombardment, the danger was by no means past. In the first chaotic postwar years cold and hunger took a heavy toll among the Germans.

In the first months after the end of the fighting the needs of the civilian population were of course at their greatest. Very little could be done to improve their lot since not only all private travel but also the parcel post and mail service to the defeated countries had been halted. Considerable time elapsed before the various aid efforts such as CARE were organized and offered an opportunity for sending the Germans food, clothing, and other necessities of life. Meanwhile the only possibility of helping those who inhabited the bleak ruins of the Third Reich was by illegal means. Sometimes members of the Allied occupation forces could be prevailed upon, at the risk of punishment or even court-martial, to convey gifts from the exiles to their families and friends in Germany.

Many emigrant authors for personal or literary reasons wanted to return to Germany as quickly as possible. Until about 1948 they had little choice but to do so as members of the Allied armed forces. Klaus Mann was one of the exiles who, after many unsuccessful tries, had finally been accepted as a volunteer in the United States Army during the war. After spending some time in training camps he was sent to North Africa, from where in due course he proceeded to Sicily. In March 1944 he moved on to Italy. He was assigned to the Psychological Warfare Branch, which tried to wear down the fighting spirit of the German frontline troops by haranguing them with the aid of powerful loudspeakers. A year later he became a staff writer for the United States Army newspaper *Stars and Stripes*, and on 5 May 1945, three days before the end of the war in Europe, he returned to Germany as a special correspondent for this publication. For the first time in some twelve years he was on his native soil again.

At the end of September Klaus Mann was discharged from the army. In the intervening five months his journalistic assignments gave him a unique opportunity to observe conditions all over Germany at first hand. He interviewed many of the German military who had been taken prisoner by the Allies. He also talked with some prominent Nazis, including Hermann Goering, who had fallen into the hands of the Americans. Mann was appalled by the attitude of many of the people he met. He noted a widespread feeling that the capitulation of Germany was merely a stratagem to prepare the way for a joint German-American offensive against the Russians.

Some of the Germans that Klaus Mann came in contact with still openly adhered to fascist views, although the vast majority insisted that they had never really been in sympathy with the Nazi movement and had not known anything about the atrocities it had committed. Those who could not deny that they had actively supported the regime usually claimed they were forced to collaborate. A striking case in point was that of the well-known actor Emil Jannings. He had abused his very popular talents to make such scurrilously anti-Semitic movies as *Jew Suess* (*Jud Süß*). To Klaus Mann, the actor asserted plaintively that he and his family would have starved to death if he had not undertaken these assignments he now pretended to despise. His opulent life style as one of the pampered favorites of the ruling Nazi clique sharply contradicted his crocodile tears and protestations of innocence.

Klaus Mann was even more disheartened by his experience in interviewing Richard Strauss. When the discussion turned to the question of exile, the aged composer declared that he had seen absolutely no reason for leaving Germany during the Hitler era. He proudly pointed out that the Nazi authorities had liked his operas and that he had earned very substantial royalties from the many performances that took place in the Third Reich. Strauss lacked any notion of the ethical issues involved. He was apparently totally unaware that he had helped shore up a corrupt regime by enabling it to maintain a thin veneer of culture.

As a protégé of the Nazi rulers Strauss had hardly been aware that there was a war going on. Some minor restrictions had been placed on his Jewish daughter-in-law's horse riding habits, but apart from that he had only one complaint against the Hitler regime. Toward the end of the war when the Allies stepped up their bombing raids, many people had been evacuated from the cities. The authorities had tried to billet some of these homeless people on the composer's large country estate. Through his personal ties with the highest party circles this threat to his privacy and comfort had at the last moment been averted. Even so, the very idea still filled him with indignation as he told Klaus Mann about it.

A similarly total, callous disregard for the civilian victims of the air war was displayed by Ernst Wiechert, one of the most prominent representatives of the literary "inner emigration." After the end of the war, when he was required to take in some evacuees on his extensive grounds, he became so incensed that he immediately sold the property. Wiechert then settled in Switzerland where until his death in 1950 he could enjoy the royalties of the books he had published in Nazi Germany, without being confronted with the victims of the regime he had thus supported.

During the tour of duty as a *Stars and Stripes* reporter in postwar Germany, Klaus Mann also revisited his family's former home in Munich. Behind the still more or less intact façade the house was in ruins. But he discovered that a young woman had improvised a shelter among the debris. She told Klaus Mann, whose identity and connection with the house she did not suspect, that the place used to belong to some writer. She thought he had been forced to leave the country because, as she put it, he was probably a Jew or something else was wrong with him. Later on the building had been used as a "Well of Life" ("Lebensborn"), a kind of human studfarm where specially selected SS men begat children with maidens of the officially approved Nordic type for the greater glory of the Teutonic race and the future strength of the German army.

About one year after Klaus Mann obtained his discharge from
the American army in Paris, another notable figure from the
world of exile literature arrived in Germany. When the war in
Europe ended, Carl Zuckmayer for largely personal reasons was
also very eager to return to his country of origin as quickly as
possible. He was at the time still settled on his farm in Vermont.
It proved to be a very involved and lengthy process to realize his
ambition. He succeeded, with much difficulty and the aid of
some influential American friends, in being appointed as an advisor for cultural affairs with the United States Army. In this
capacity he worked for several months in a New York office,
translating and interpreting reports from Germany by men in the
field. Finally after much prodding he managed to be sent over
there himself under orders to assess the cultural situation in postwar Germany and to make suggestions for its improvement and
stimulation.

The conditions under which Zuckmayer could carry out his
assignment were extremely favorable. He held the rank of captain
and enjoyed all the privileges and benefits of his officer's status,
including a salary that by European standards was astronomical,
but he was not required to wear the army uniform. This freedom
to wear civilian clothes was of great importance in establishing
frank and cordial relations with the Germans. Even when they
were not intimidated by the uniform of an officer of the occupation forces, they might in many cases well have harbored some
suspicions about Zuckmayer's motives in joining the American
army.

His experiences in Germany were on the whole more encourag-
ing than those of Klaus Mann had been. The nature and circumstances of Zuckmayer's assignment and the time that had elapsed
since Mann made his observations account for much of the difference between their respective impressions. Zuckmayer found
that the public still fondly remembered his pre-Nazi work. His
new play *The Devil's General* (*Des Teufels General*) during this time
received its first performance in Zurich and was a resounding success with both the public and the critics. Such things naturally
raised Zuckmayer's hopes for the future of Europe. In other
respects he also had some reason to take a less somber view than

Klaus Mann of the German people, their past and their prospects. His old and ailing parents had during the final stages of the war been threatened with deportation, but they had been saved from this fate and certain death by the humane and kind attitude of one of the Nazi officials with whom they came in contact.

But in spite of such experiences and of his generally positive impressions, Carl Zuckmayer's return to his native land was not a uniformly happy occasion. His joy at meeting old friends and his hopes for the future were overshadowed by the realization that he really no longer had a country. Although he had been quite happy on his farm in Vermont, he still was very much aware of being a newcomer in America who had no personal or cultural roots there. Having tried earlier to make some money by writing short fiction in English, he was especially conscious of a formidable language barrier. As a writer he would always need the German tongue as his expressive medium. In other respects he found himself upon his return to the country of his birth alienated from the German people. The spectre of the Nazi years always stood between him as a returning exile and those who had spent the Hitler years in Germany. The mentality and the experiences of the emigrant were fundamentally incompatible with the outlook even of unyielding antifascists who had remained in the country. In that sense there was no return for the exile.

Alfred Döblin was another exile author who became painfully aware of the gulf that had opened between himself and his compatriots. He returned to Germany in November 1945 as an officer in the French occupation force. Döblin was stationed in the southeastern resort town of Baden-Baden where he became involved in French-German cultural affairs. His desire to contribute to a revival of literary life in Germany prompted him to found a new journal. He successfully overcame the most formidable difficulties and shortages to launch *Das goldene Tor*, the first publication of its kind to appear in the Western occupation zones. The journal was dedicated to the venerable liberal-humanistic tradition that had played such a large role in exile literature. But it soon became apparent that in postwar Germany this attitude was no longer viable. For lack of public response *Das goldene Tor* soon ceased to exist, and by 1953 Döblin had become so thoroughly disillusioned with conditions in West Germany that once again he emigrated and settled in Paris.

Part of his disenchantment and that of others in the immediate postwar years was due to the almost total stagnation of literary life from 1945 until 1947. The disarray of the mail service and public transportation, the collapse of the monetary system, the lack of paper, and the war damage to many printing plants made it all but impossible to publish anything. It was in fact not until the currency reform of June 1948 that material conditions improved to the point where any kind of cultural activity became possible again. Even then the returned exiles found themselves in almost all cases greatly frustrated in their ambitions and attempts to contribute their share to the reconstruction of German writing.

In their long years abroad they had often kept up their spirits with the prospect that after the war they would be called upon to save their country's cultural heritage. Now that the time had come they were met with suspicion and rejection by a large section of the populace. Most of the writers who had stayed in Germany under the fascists denounced the former emigrants as traitors and deserters. Especially those who had adopted the "inner emigration" tag to justify and explain their own decision to remain in the country were openly and bitterly hostile toward the exile writers. They focused their attack on the symbolic head of the literary emigration, Thomas Mann.

Mann's wartime series of monthly radio talks to the German people over the British Broadcasting Corporation had aroused the anger of many of his listeners. He had tried to open their eyes to the true nature of the Hitler regime and to spur them on to at least passive resistance. The Germans largely considered his tone and attitude toward his former country to be vindictive and hostile. In the address of 8 May 1945 Thomas Mann made some statements that considerably widened the rift between him and his audience. Allied troops had just penetrated to the German concentration and extermination camps and had discovered the full extent of their horrors. Mann called the existence of these camps a disgrace for all Germans and remarked that the moral fiber of the people had been corrupted by the Nazi regime. He also observed that the Germans had not been able to rid themselves of their fascist overlords—the country had had to be liberated from the outside. Mann concluded that the Allies would have to rule and administer Germany for years to come. His speech was afterward printed in a Bavarian newspaper. This increased the impact of his words on the German people considerably, but there was no immediate response. Because of the shortages and restrictions under which the media were laboring it took almost three months before there was any public reaction.

The aging author Walter von Molo had spent the war years in Germany as a rather typical representative of the "inner emigration." On 13 August 1945 he addressed Thomas Mann with an open letter in the *Münchner Zeitung*. Molo rejected the idea of a collective responsibility of the German people as a whole for the misdeeds and crimes of their rulers, saying that the man in the street fundamentally had nothing in common with the sick minds that had conceived and committed the "shameful horrors and lies and the terrible mistakes" that had culminated in the death camps. Walter von Molo also criticized Thomas Mann's comment on the necessity for the conquerors to govern Germany for a long time to come. Molo associated this notion with the humiliating and ineffective denazification and reeducation programs of the Allies, but his attitude toward Mann was strangely paradoxical. He disagreed with the exiled writer on these basic issues, yet at the same time he apparently shared the opinion of numerous emigrants that Thomas Mann had the authority and personal status to play a leading role in the political life of the shattered nation. The open letter contained an appeal to Mann to return to Germany soon "like a good physician who does not only see the facts but looks for the causes of the diseases." He was challenged to contribute in a public capacity to the reestablishment of the country.

A few days after the appearance of Walter von Molo's open letter, the same newspaper published an essay on the subject of "inner emigration." It was written by Frank Thiess, a minor writer who in 1933 had publicly praised Hitler. In the context of an attempt to justify his own collaboration with the Nazis, Thiess supported Walter von Molo's position. He attacked the view held by Thomas Mann and many other exiles that only those who had left the country had offered effective opposition to the fascists. Thiess claimed that he had derived a deeper human and spiritual experience by staying in Germany than would have resulted from observing the "German tragedy" from abroad. Apart from such criticism of the exile movement in general, he also aimed specifically for Thomas Mann. In an obvious allusion to the famous novelist, Thiess asserted that it was more difficult to preserve the integrity of one's personality in Hitler Germany than to send messages to its people from across the border.

Thomas Mann took his time in answering these charges and invitations. It was not until almost two months after the publications by Molo and Thiess that he responded. On 12 October 1945, an article under the title "Why I Don't Return" appeared in an Augsburg paper. In it Mann referred to the physical and psychological hardships of exile. He accused those who had remained in Germany of a lack of solidarity that had reduced the effectiveness of the exiles' opposition to Nazism. Mann went on to point out that he had become a United States citizen and had good reason to be grateful to his new country. On the other hand he felt estranged from Germany and therefore had no intention of returning.

Thomas Mann tried to spare his readers' feelings as much as possible. He linked his refusal to come back to Germany with an expression of faith in its future. He also claimed to feel himself bound to his country of birth by unbreakable emotional ties. But as he had anticipated, the Germans registered only the rejection of their invitation, and they reacted with considerable hostility. Even so, Mann's decision not to return was not the most controversial issue at stake; another statement of his caused a greater uproar and brought the conflict to a head. Mann had offered some observations on the literature that had been produced in the Third Reich including the writings of the "inner emigration," pointing out that the Nazis had used all artistic and literary activity in their domain as a façade for Hitler's regime. He therefore condemned everything that had been printed in Germany with the consent of the fascists as being less than worthless. According to Mann it was tainted with "a smell of blood and shame." He added that all the books concerned should be pulped.

This emotional comment provided his adversaries with an opportunity that they did not miss. Toward the end of October a Berlin newspaper printed a contribution by art historian and professor Edwin Redslob in which Thomas Mann's words were twisted to imply that the novelist had advocated burning the literature of the "inner emigration." In this way Mann could be discredited by associating him with the Nazi book burnings. Redslob's article, and others, also denied Mann the right to judge and condemn the writing of those who had spent the Nazi era in Germany. He should first acquire a deeper understanding of the literature and the circumstances under which it had come into being.

Selfishness was imputed to Mann as the main motivation for his refusal to return to Germany. There were angry denials that his opinions, as Walter von Molo had indicated, mattered to the Germans. The novelist's refusal to accept a position of leadership was regarded by many as an insult, so that voices were raised to the effect that he had totally alienated himself from his country of origin and had lost all influence. His pronouncements were said to be offered from a position of loneliness and incapable of arousing an echo among the public.

The fairly well known author Otto Flake joined in the debate with some curious comments. He thought that Thomas Mann could have waited a bit longer before becoming an American citizen if he really had believed that Hitler would be defeated. This observation completely and conveniently overlooked the fact that Mann had first been deprived of his German citizenship by the Nazi authorities. Flake advanced another peculiar argument to the effect that the Germans had picked the chestnuts out of the fire for humanity in general, by demonstrating the dangers of totalitarianism.

In the avalanche of abuse and hostility that was now unleashed, the few reasonable voices were easy to overhear. Wilhelm Hausenstein for instance struck a moderate, conciliatory note in an article in the *Süddeutsche Zeitung* of 24 December 1945. Hausenstein admitted that all books published with the permission of the Nazis to some extent served their cause. At the same time he postulated a duty on the part of the authors to cater to the public's need for works of genuine literary value. The writers had an obligation to fulfill this function in spite of the fact that the regime exploited their books for propaganda purposes. Hausenstein also took a moderate stand in connection with Thomas Mann's excessively sweeping condemnation of "inner emigration" writing. He listed a number of works from that category that according to him had both literary and ideological merit.

Thomas Mann did not let himself be drawn into a direct polemic with his detractors. Instead, in a broadcast of 30 December 1945, he reaffirmed his decision not to return to Germany. On this same occasion he again expressed his dismay that seventy million Germans had not been able to get rid of the Hitler clique in the six years between its rise to power and the outbreak of the war. As he remarked, the people as a whole had on the contrary done everything in their power to win the fascists' war and to perpetuate their regime. He also pointed out some discrepancies in the arguments earlier advanced by Frank Thiess. That very same day, Thiess was given an opportunity to respond on the North German radio. In an insinuating and patronizing tone he repeated his earlier claim that Mann had become isolated because he did not share the German people's intimate experience of Nazism. He accused the exile writer once again of arrogance, insolence, and a lack of love and respect.

Encouraged by this and similar utterances, the tone of the continuing attacks against Thomas Mann became more and more vicious. In January 1946 someone publicly thanked Frank Thiess for his comments, repeating his arguments in scurrilous and aggressive terms and adding that Mann was being ungrateful toward his fatherland. The egocentricity of these "inner emigration" champions manifested itself in the contention that the Nazi experience had had a deeply humanizing effect on them, which had supposedly made them morally superior to Thomas Mann. The suffering and death of millions of Nazi victims were apparently irrelevant to these people, who seemed interested only in the presumed benefit to their own personalities.

Early in 1946 Johannes Becher, who had recently returned from his exile in Moscow, wrote a private letter to Frank Thiess on the subject. Becher agreed that some of Thomas Mann's expressed views were "puzzling," but he warned Thiess against those who jumped on his bandwagon to attack the novelist in a style reminiscent of the most vicious Nazi slander campaigns. Thiess reacted vehemently to this well-meant, sensible letter. In his response he took his previous line of argument to extremes of aggressiveness and illogicality, repeating the charge that Thomas Mann was infected with the spirit of National Socialism.

Thiess also took issue with Mann's reproach about the Germans' failure to rebel against Hitler. Although Mann had referred specifically to the period from 1933 to 1939, Thiess based his argument on the German wartime occupation of almost all of Europe. He defended the Germans' lack of resistance against Hitler by saying that the people in the German-occupied countries had not risen against the invaders either. To his way of thinking that argument was all the stronger for the fact that the able-bodied men in these territories had not—like the Germans —been inducted into the army. What Thiess did not mention in this connection was that most of the German soldiers were stationed in the occupied countries precisely in order to suppress any attempt at an uprising on the part of the population. He furthermore implicitly absolved the Germans from all guilt for the Nazi era and its terror by speaking of the "inescapable and fate-willed German catastrophe." Such formulations tend to shift the responsibility from the human realm to the level of cosmic forces.

The attacks on Thomas Mann also included efforts to discredit his personal integrity. In May 1947 the fairly popular writer Manfred Hausmann published an article entitled "Thomas Mann Should Keep Silent." He claimed that Mann about one year after he had taken up residence in Switzerland had petitioned the Nazis to be allowed to return to Germany. When challenged to prove his allegation, Hausmann produced a letter from Mann of 2 April 1934, applying for a renewal of his passport in order not to become stateless by default. In the same document Mann had also protested against the confiscation of his house, library, and other possessions by the Nazis. There was nothing in the letter to support the charge that the novelist had sought to come to terms with the fascists. When his slander had been exposed as totally unfounded, Hausmann lamely explained that he had attempted the character assassination for the purpose of curbing Thomas Mann's influence.

As the public controversy raged on, many Germans, including those who at first had been on Thomas Mann's side, turned against him. This became clear when in July 1949 he visited Germany for the first time in sixteen years. He was given a cool if not downright unfriendly reception. He made even more enemies in West Germany when following his visit there he went to the eastern sector of the country, where he was honored by the Communist functionaries. Upon his return to the United States, Mann found that his journey to East Germany was taken amiss by both the authorities and the general public. Coming on top of his persistent refusal to subscribe to the mounting anti-Communist campaign, this demonstration of open-mindedness was widely regarded with suspicion. In the prevailing atmosphere of political paranoia, Mann suddenly became so unpopular that a long-planned speech at the Library of Congress was summarily canceled. The German-American press had meanwhile also joined in the attacks on him. The *Neue Volks-Zeitung* for instance had before and during the war always loudly sung his praises, but as early as 1947 it reflected the changing times with the publication of a polemical contribution by leading socialist journalist Friedrich Stampfer. Echoing "inner emigration" sentiments, he called Thomas Mann a "retired apostle of humanity" and accused him of lacking "nobility of heart."

More hostile articles followed in this and other German-American publications. In the United States the antagonism toward Thomas Mann reached its climax during the era of Senator Joseph McCarthy and the more notorious activities of the House Un-American Activities Committee. To Mann the criticism leveled against him personally was only a symptom of a general deterioration of the American political climate. The prevailing trends in public life since the end of the war seemed to negate everything that his hero President Roosevelt had stood for. His disillusionment and loss of public status were felt all the keener by the aging novelist because of his increasing personal isolation. Many fellow exiles had returned to Europe and a number of his close friends had died. He stuck to his decision not to go back to

Germany, but in July 1952 Mann left America and settled in the German-speaking part of Switzerland, near the city of Zurich.

During the three years of life that remained to him he received numerous honors. To some extent they made up for the insults and indignities he had endured in the controversies with the "inner emigration" and with his erstwhile admirers in America. But at the same time, the recognition that now came his way signaled a change in his public image. He was no longer regarded as an active combatant in the ongoing ideological and literary battles. The laurels that Mann gathered in the final years of his life stamped him as a monument, if not a relic, of a bygone era, who was no longer a factor to be reckoned with and could therefore safely be honored. From this perspective, Mann's "rehabilitation" in the general estimation proved that he, and with him the literary emigration, had ultimately failed to inspire and fertilize postwar writing with the faithfully and conscientiously preserved traditions of pre-Nazi Germany.

11
The Aftermath

Living among ruins, clothed in rags, stealing, begging, and bartering scraps of food and a few lumps of coal, the people in postwar Germany were engaged in a merciless battle for bare survival. Nevertheless for all the material misery there was a tremendous upsurge of public interest in all art forms including literature. The twelve years of Nazi censorship had smothered all creativity in its inevitable ethical and aesthetic corruption. But it soon became obvious that for the eastern part of the country, which at the end of the war was under Russian occupation and in 1949 became the German Democratic Republic, the change of regime did not substantially alter the situation. The new state controlled literary life even more rigorously than the Nazis had, prescribing both form and content of the works that were permitted to be published.

Under these circumstances, the faithful Communist Party members among the writers in exile found a warm welcome in East Germany, and some of them in time rose to high positions in the political hierarchy. Their works were promoted with all the means at the government's disposal, and so these former emigrants soon became highly popular. They did not of course have much competition, since books from Western Europe were almost totally banned, especially in the first postwar years, while the Party-inspired new "talent" ground out only the most dismal social-realist novels about production quotas, hymns to Stalin, and similar things.

While the doctrinaire Communist writers fit smoothly into the official and cultural climate of East Germany, the other political sectors of the literary emigration found themselves out of step with the mood in the western part of the country. There the people avidly pursued the possibilities of unfettered expression that the first years of peace in a kind of fresh start euphoria seemed to promise. Under these circumstances it was doubtful that exile literature, even without the mud-slinging of the "inner emigration," would have been able to inspire and shape a new phase in West German writing. The literary emigration's lack of resonance in postwar West Germany was also due at least in part to the characteristic ideological and artistic obsolescence of the authors. Exiles almost always tend to cling to the views and ideals on whose account they have been banished. The non-Communist wing of the antifascist literary emigration was in this respect highly typical. The authors remained politically and stylistically caught up in the early thirties. In their long difficult years of exile they had sustained themselves intellectually with the hope that the ideological and artistic principles that originally marked them as opponents of fascism would be rehabilitated and eventually reinstated in a free Germany.

After the war a restorative attitude like this was simply not viable. The old ideals had lost their popular appeal during the long Hitler years. They did not take into account the tremendous impact of the Second World War on Europe and indeed the whole world. The people's views had changed drastically under the experiences of a decade and a half of turmoil and war. Most of the emigrant authors continued to subscribe to ideologies that ranged from liberal-humanistic to anarchist, with a preponderance of doctrinaire socialism. These political persuasions after 1945 seemed distinctly archaic, arousing unwelcome memories of the Weimar Republic in the throes of the Great Depression with all its unrest, discontent, and poverty. How remote from prevailing popular sentiment the exile writers' orientation was in this regard is clearly demonstrated by the long tenure of the unabashedly capitalist laissez-faire regime of Chancellor Adenauer and economics minister Erhard from 1948 until 1963.[1]

But if the exiles had fallen behind the times, the "inner emigration" also failed dismally to establish itself as a guiding force in post war Germany. In the relentlessly cold light of the dawning new era, the representatives of this political twilight zone were found to be wanting. Their attitude was too vaguely idealistic and their language too reminiscent of the turgid prose of Nazi propaganda. To the German public they were unacceptable as ideological or literary leaders. They disappointed their former fans by failing to produce even a single work of truly inspiring quality. Contrary to widespread expectations not one of them came forth with unpublished masterpieces written during the Nazi years that might have launched a new period in German letters.

And so while the champions of exile literature and "inner emigration" were at each others' throats over the question who was better qualified to dominate the prospective literary life in Germany, both lost out to a third faction that had its roots in the German prisoner of war camps in America and more specifically in some of the publications put out by the inmates. The various camp journals represented a wide range of aesthetic and political opinion, from mysticism and irrationalism to sober analysis and criticism. Some were imbued with a nationalistic and militaristic spirit that expressed itself mainly in texts in praise of war as an intensified state of existence. This writing tended to be traditional in form and style.

The youth movements of the twenties were echoed in other POW journals that emphasized an idyllic nature concept and preached the virtues of family life. The authors and editors concerned had a somewhat provincial notion of literary values. They had pinned their hopes for the future of German letters on the "inner emigration," with which they had a pronounced ideational affinity. A third major group of camp publications subscribed to a viewpoint that may best be characterized as liberal and antifascist. The representatives of this current strove to be as cosmopolitan in their literary tastes as the youth movement enthusiasts were provincial. These progressives among the prisoners tended to stress the democratic aspects of their German heritage. For want of more recent untarnished idols they dwelt on the struggle against tyranny and absolutism by the eighteenth-century dramatist Friedrich Schiller. Another source of inspiration was found in the vain attempts of the Young Germans in the early nineteenth century to infuse the spirit of the French Revolution into German political life.

Different elements had gone into the making of the liberals' intellectual and creative attitudes: existentialism and skepticism, Christian and Marxist ideas, a tendency toward apocalyptic visions and a defeatist streak. From these often contradictory impulses sprang the movement that for nearly twenty years was to set the tone of German writing. Toward the end of the war a number of the more influential representatives of this progressive wing were brought together in a particular camp. They had been selected by the American authorities for special training in preparation for the planned reeducation and denazification programs. They included a number of seasoned publicists and contributors to the various liberal POW journals. With the cooperation of the Americans, they now founded a new publication called *Der Ruf*, intended for distribution in all POW camps. The journal appeared in this original form during the years 1945 and 1946 when speculation about the political future of Germany was at its height. *Der Ruf*'s captive readership was of course especially preoccupied with this question.

In this situation it was only natural that the publication went out of its way to stimulate the readers' ideological sophistication, trying to promote a critical, rational outlook based on the principle of individual responsibility. This editorial orientation did not fit in at all with the collectivistic aspect of Marxism. By the same token the journal's policy leaned strongly toward Freudian and existentialist views. *Der Ruf* also subscribed wholeheartedly to President Roosevelt's "one world" concept of universal peace based on a synthesis of democracy and socialism. Germany would have a vital role to play in the realization of this plan as a mediator between East and West.

Its preoccupation with political matters determined the journal's position in regard to literature. It was not seen primarily in aesthetic terms but rather as a means of publicizing and disseminating ideological opinions and convictions. As a result of this attitude *Der Ruf* fostered the genre of the essay, for instance, which otherwise was rather neglected in German letters. So far as creative fiction writing was concerned, the editors adopted as their favorite models such authors as Hemingway and Steinbeck. Their presumably plain, concretely objective prose was considered worthy of emulation.

Of the contemporary German writers few found favor in the eyes of *Der Ruf*. In its judgment the exiles in their anxiety to preserve their literary heritage had arrived at "formalistic dead ends." The "inner emigration" was considered an essentially nineteenth-century form of bourgeois humanism, and its representatives were on the whole written off as irrelevant and ineffective. Somewhat incongruously, the leading figure of the movement, Ernst Jünger, was not included in its general condemnation. Like many others the prospective leaders of the new German world of letters failed to see through the fake heroism of *On the Marble Cliffs* to its crypto-fascist core.

One of the editors of *Der Ruf*, Alfred Andersch, called the work "breathtaking" and described it as a "unique work of art" of "somber beauty." And probably under the impact of Jünger's novel, Andersch reiterated the "inner emigration" claim that their Nazi approved publications had not helped the fascists but rather had served to undermine their regime. In this connection Andersch postulated generously that all literature written during the Hitler period was anti-Nazi and therefore belonged at least mentally to the emigration. To back up this tortuous argument he simply decreed that pro-Nazi writing did not belong to the realm of literature.

In 1946 Andersch and his fellow editor Hans Werner Richter, having been released from the POW camp, returned to Germany, where they founded a new version of *Der Ruf* to help translate into practice the ideas formulated in their American captivity. Specifically they advocated what Richter called the literary style of "magic realism," which combined radical objectivity of expression with a montage technique that sought to evoke the essential by omitting it. The term itself indicates *Der Ruf*'s cosmopolitan orientation, having been coined by the protean Italian author Massimo Bontempelli. The journal was also open to other influences from abroad. Early in 1947 it somewhat changed its editorial direction in accordance with certain impulses that originated from the former anti-Nazi resistance movement in France. The resulting existentialist bias gave rise to the notion of a radically new beginning "from scratch" or as it was also called, from a "zero point" ("Nullpunkt") at which all traditions had lost their validity.

The American authorities in charge of press licenses in their occupation zone regarded the existentialism adopted by *Der Ruf* as a form of nihilism. They were afraid these ideas might not be conducive to the Germans' reeducation and therefore in April 1947 withdrew the journal's permit. This step was taken all the more readily since *Der Ruf* had continued to advocate Roosevelt's "one world" idea, and such a synthesis of liberty and socialism was no longer in keeping with the political climate in America as it had developed since FDR's death.

When *Der Ruf* was banned Hans Werner Richter immediately developed plans for a new journal to take its place, which was to be called *Der Skorpion*. A dummy issue was prepared for discussion by the major prospective contributors who came together for this purpose in Munich. While they were gathered there, the American military government turned down the application for a publication permit for *Der Skorpion*. The authors then decided to read aloud to each other the texts they had brought with them for the stillborn publication. This led to an impromptu discussion and an outspoken critical analysis of each other's work.

Because conditions in Germany at the time were still so chaotic that the writers could seldom communicate or gather together, they worked very much in isolation. The freewheeling mutual comments at their Munich meeting under these circumstances proved to be a very stimulating experience. To compensate for the failure of *Der Skorpion* they decided to make an annual event of their get-together. Under this arrangement the Group '47 (Gruppe '47), as they called themselves, set the tone in West German literature during the following twenty-odd years. At the yearly meetings the foundation members and those newcomers who were invited by Hans Werner Richter exposed themselves and their writings to each other's instant criticism. Those who survived this ordeal usually went on to a successful literary career and before long the German world of letters was firmly dominated by Group '47. But the influence and prestige that this loosely constituted body wielded inevitably led to commercialization, and by the mid-sixties the annual gatherings had deteriorated into publicity spectaculars manipulated by several astute publishers.

Before eventually outliving its usefulness and reputation, Group '47 did much to liberate German writing from its long standing and ingrained tendency toward provincialism and woolly-mindedness. It staunchly championed—at least in theory—a sophisticated, cosmopolitan attitude toward literature. The group scornfully rejected everything that smacked of pseudoromanticism or expressionistic regurgitations. Through the years its own ideals and objectives changed considerably; the initial fascination with Hemingway for instance grew noticeably less from about 1949 on. But Group '47 always remained faithful to the notion that literature was not an aesthetic end in itself. It steadfastly adhered to the doctrine that writing was a social phenomenon and as such ultimately subordinate to the political sphere.

This insistence on the primacy of agitation and propaganda was the exact opposite of the attitude held by most of the non-Communist exile authors, who had only rather reluctantly under the inescapable pressure of circumstances politicized their writing. Whereas Group '47 had as its ultimate aim the establishment of a new socioeconomic order, the emigrants had basically opposed the fascists in order to restore a cultural climate in which an aesthetically oriented literature could once again thrive.

12
A Stone Fiddle

When after the 1948 currency reform West Germany overcame the chaos and devastation of the lost war, the intellectual atmosphere changed rapidly. The people's initial eagerness to catch up with the rest of the world after fifteen years of isolation gave way to a more contemplative mood. But this development did not make the cultural climate more receptive or congenial to the non-Communist exile writers. As the "economic miracle" took effect the public's new sense of accomplishment and security allowed it to indulge in the luxury of nostalgia. The twenties became an object of bemused interest, and in the years that followed the work of many authors from that period was reprinted and revived. The exile authors had been rooted in that same period, but very few of them shared in this upsurge of popularity, and the literary emigration as a movement was almost entirely excluded from it.

This is partly explained by the political winds that blew ever stronger in the Federal Republic of Germany. As the memories of the Third Reich receded into the past, it too came to be regarded with a certain tolerance. Reversely, it became more and more of a liability in politics as in literature to have been an antifascist exile.[1] But disturbing though this aspect of the continued neglect of exile literature is, it should not be overlooked that there were other factors at work as well. It was not only political antagonism that for some two decades after the end of the war kept the major part of the books written in exile from being published in West Germany. At least as important was the often rather poor quality of the writing, which Menno ter Braak had criticized as early as 1934.

The circumstances of their exile had forced the writers to become increasingly political in much of their work, as direct activism and propaganda against the Nazis were widely thought to be the primary functions of emigration literature. But by subordinating their creativity to the antifascist endeavor, the authors fell prey to the inherent aesthetic pitfalls of political writing. As a result exile literature was generally found not only ideologically unappealing, but also artistically inadequate.[2]

However, those exile works that were not immediately or pronouncedly political in nature tended to be flawed as well. Many things contributed to this state of affairs, including the effects of material misery and poor living conditions. Even more to the point was the fact that the expressive medium itself had become problematical for the exiled writers. For many of them the awareness that the Nazis used the German tongue for their hate propaganda against political opponents and racial victims degraded and debilitated the language. These writers felt that the fascists had perverted their creative medium and turned it into an "instrument of tyrannical rage."

The most uncompromising view on the matter was that the German language in all its manifestations had been dishonored and discredited through its demagogic abuse in Germany and therefore was no longer a viable vehicle for any kind of honest writing. In fact from this perspective, German had become the language of guilt, and anyone who used it thereby shared in that guilt. The proponents of this view left themselves no option but to give up their literary activity altogether. Even aside from such emotional inhibitions, the emigrant authors all suffered the detrimental effects of being cut off from their own expressive medium. In their places of refuge they increasingly lost touch with the living language, and their creative command of it consequently became less and less sure. Their mastery of German deteriorated not only because they were removed from its actual, vital origin but also as a result of contamination and interference by their new linguistic environment.

Peter Weiss, for example, had as a young man migrated to Sweden with his parents. There he tried to record his earlier experiences as a victim of Nazi racism and persecution but found to his dismay that he ran into insoluble difficulties in the use of his childhood language. With a great effort of will and concentration he could shut out from his mind the language that surrounded him in his exile. Even so, those things that he wanted to say could not be expressed adequately because the German tongue had lost its natural communicative function for him. It had become the language of the enemy. Writing in it Weiss could no longer maintain the essential assumption that he was addressing a receptive public. His expressive ability was stifled by the feeling that on the contrary those who understood the language should not know what he wrote about and against them. As a result his style became awkward and lifeless, and his words lacked any deeper evocative relation to the ideas and experiences that he attempted to note down.

It was a very common experience among the exiles, that their German tended to become a shadow of its former self. Many exiles tried to convince themselves that the gradual emasculation of their language was really a process of refinement, a view advanced very vigorously by Lion Feuchtwanger. He chose to regard the increasing lifelessness of his German as the result of conscious stylization. After some ten years of exile he commented on the "bitter experience of being separated from the living stream of the mother tongue." But as far as his own work was concerned, he reconciled himself with this state of affairs and even came to look upon it in a positive light. His increasing estrangement from the German language as spoken by the people made his own style increasingly artificial and abstract, but rather than be alarmed by the deterioration of his German expression he prided himself on its supposed objectivity.

While Feuchtwanger deceived himself when he welcomed the gradual impoverishment of his language as conscious artistry, in some few instances the effects of the prolonged exile on a writer's expressive capacity were not detrimental. Thomas Mann and Bertolt Brecht for instance also incorporated something of the emigrants' typical linguistic artificiality in their styles. Their cases were in fact exceptional in that their creative attitudes were consistent with the somewhat stilted language forced upon them by their exiled state. The novelist's "irony" and the playwright's "alienation" principle were vastly different in method and effect. Yet both were marked by an unusually distant epic stance and therefore thrived on the progressive abstraction of the authors' German.[3]

These two writers virtually alone among the ranks of the literary emigration found their styles enhanced rather than debilitated by their linguistic isolation. It is certainly no mere coincidence that they were also the first eventually to become accepted by the German public. After the bitterness aroused by the "inner emigration" campaign against Mann had somewhat subsided and the political implications of Brecht's plays no longer obscured their artistic significance, both authors came to be recognized as major literary figures. But even when they were widely accepted as writers of the first rank, their participation in the antifascist exile movement was effectively ignored.

That this was possible, that their work could be separated from its biographical association with the emigration, was probably a prerequisite for their belated popularity. It depended on the stylistic and conceptual distance with which they treated their subject matter, including exile and anti-Nazi topics. This same cognitive elevation above the theme also accounts for the fact that retrospective visions of the Hitler era have been much in demand. Works such as Günter Grass's 1959 novel *The Tin Drum* (*Die Blechtrommel*) and Siegfried Lenz's *German Lesson* (*Die Deutschstunde*) of 1968 received massive popular acclaim. But exile writing continued to languish in a virtual limbo, with the exception only of those few authors who stylistically sublimated their topic.

The link between critical recognition, artistic quality, and breadth of perspective is further demonstrated in the case of Nelly Sachs, who also received belated acclaim for her work. In 1965 she was given the coveted Peace Prize of the German book-trade, and in 1966 she was awarded the Nobel Prize for literature. Before the war, as the unmarried daughter of a well-to-do, thoroughly assimilated Jewish industrialist in Berlin, she dabbled in writing. Through her literary interest she had at a very early age already won the friendship of the famous Swedish writer Selma Lagerlöf, a connection that eventually saved her life.

Most of her relatives and friends were killed by the Nazis, but thanks to the combined efforts of the Swedish novelist and the King of Sweden, Nelly Sachs in May 1940 was permitted to leave Germany with her mother.[4] This experience proved to be a decisive turning point in the life and the career of the then almost fifty-year-old poet. From this time on she specifically regarded herself as the spokesman of her people. She tended to view the events of her time from a historical perspective as the culmination of a long tradition of persecution. It became her conviction that she had been physically saved to fulfill her mission of expressing the suffering and fate of the Jews in her poetry. In this connection she characterized the nature and the motivation of her creativity with the words "Death was my teacher."

Being persecuted because of her "race" rather than her politics, Nelly Sachs in adopting a representative stance and a historical perspective in essence renounced the country of her birth. The loss of her homeland was a deep emotional trauma, the more so since she remained dependent on the German language as her artistic medium. Another exiled Jewish poet, Karl Wolfskehl, reacted to this dilemma by postulating that his only true home, from which he could not be expelled, was the word. Nelly Sachs in this situation adopted neither a linguistic nor a political substitute for her lost country of origin; instead she found compensation in the realm of mystical contemplation.

Her outlook was expressed in the lines that she selected as the motto for one of her major poetry collections: "In place of the homeland / I hold the transmutations of the world" ("An Stelle von Heimat / halte ich die Verwandlungen der Welt"). This formulation, cryptic though it may be, contains the key to her thought. The word "transmutation" is a technical term from the Gnostic tradition and Nelly Sach's use of it indicates that she had embraced this form of Jewish mysticism. The insight at which the Gnostics aimed was to be the result of divine inspiration. It was to be achieved through the direct contemplation of God. This quest for esoteric knowledge about the other world took different forms, including cabalistic mysticism as developed in the *Sohar*. There are indications that Nelly Sachs was familiar with this thirteenth-century text and consciously incorporated elements from its teachings in her own writing.

The concept of "transmutation" expresses the notion that the universe is constantly evolving and changing. Consequently it offers man no security or permanence and no home in the sense of a fixed center of his existence. In this idea Nelly Sachs's fate as an emigrant and her expulsion from the world she had regarded as her own is absorbed by the ancient mystical philosophy of her people. This elevated her private existence to a symbolic level and lent her lyric language the quality of a revelation. It established contact and communication between the physical and the supernatural worlds.

In this focus the torture and death of the Jews at the hands of the Nazis was also associated with mystic concepts. One of Sachs's best-known poems for instance deals with the chimneys of the death camp crematoriums. The text speaks of "roads to freedom for the dust of Job and Jeremiah" through which the body of Israel, dissolved in smoke, escapes into the air. This is a very trenchant, graphic image of the reality of Auschwitz and Dachau. But at the same time it ties in with the precabalistic tradition of a Gnostic heavenly journey.

In the creative sublimation of Mann, Brecht, and Sachs, the antifascist theme was delivered from the transiency of political activist writing. The topic was elevated to an aesthetic level that revealed its broader implications. Lifted out of the sphere of immediate private involvement and agitatorial intent and placed in a historical and philosophical perspective, the subject matter assumed a significance beyond its own temporal and emotional bounds. In this way, in these few isolated instances, exile literature survived as a living part of contemporary culture, taking its place alongside other great artistic treatments of the eternal struggle between good and evil.

But the few exceptions merely proved the rule that the literary emigration ultimately failed as artistic expression because it was conceptually and linguistically too much a product of the passions and circumstances of its time. And while this lack of distance prevented the writing from achieving creative cogency it did not make it effective in an immediate political sense either.

Exile literature in its entirety as a political and aesthetic fiasco reconfirms the fact that artistic creation cannot be subordinated to any other perceptual perspective. In retrospect the story of the literary emigration is valuable as an object lesson that the progressive politicization of life in all its manifestations ultimately is the doom of civilization as a multifaceted synthesis of individual existences. Leonhard Frank's image of the stone fiddle turns out to be uncannily accurate. The exile writers with very few exceptions tried to play on an instrument that only superficially resembled the tool of their trade. The subtle organic material of living words with the resonance of symbol and metaphor, in their long and harrowing exile became mute as their language ossified and their vision narrowed to the immediate problems of fear and hope, destruction and survival.

Notes and Bibliography

Notes

Chapter 1

1. On this topic, see especially Hans-Albert Walter, *Deutsche Exilliteratur 1933–1950: Bedrohung und Verfolgung bis 1933*, pp. 117f. The political isolation of the intellectual middle class was not a purely German phenomenon. In Holland, Menno ter Braak in 1934 published a major essay with the revealing title *Politician Without a Party* (*Politicus zonder Partij*).

Chapter 5

1. A number of personal memoirs as well as official documents attest to the anti-Jewish bias of Swiss officialdom. Alfred A. Häsler has collected much evidence in his study *The Lifeboat is Full*.

2. Secretary Hull, Undersecretary Welles, and two lower ranking State Department officials conceived the Evian Conference for this purpose, as revealed in an undated memo on refugee problems from the Division of European affairs, attached to Division of the American Republics memo of 15 November 1938, quoted by Arthur D. Morse in *While Six Million Died*, p. 167.

Chapter 7

1. The quite inexplicable, prodigious fame that Hauptmann enjoyed during his lifetime still colors the perception of many literary scholars.

The negative view on the artistic quality of his writings expressed in this chapter is principally based on a personal value judgment which, although supportable by stylistic analysis, is still to an extent subjective and therefore open to disagreement. The critical assessment is, however, entirely in line with the outlook of such prominent scholars as Walter Muschg. Many of the biographical details cited in the following pages are derived from the section "Sonnenuntergang: Die letzten Tage Gerhart Hauptmanns" in Muschg's book *Die Zerstörung der deutschen Literatur*, but the most damning indictment against Hauptmann as a Nazi collaborator is to be found in the hallelujahs addressed to him by fascist commentators like Josef Nadler. See Nadler's "Sein Werk in der Gemeinschaft der Völker," in *Gerhart Hauptmann zum 80. Geburtstag am 15. November, 1942* (Breslau: Schlesien-Verlag, 1942).

2. Differing opinions have been voiced about the relationships with the fascist regime of many authors who remained in Germany under Hitler. Owing to his prominence, the case of Ernst Jünger has been particularly hotly debated. The view represented here is among others supported by the eminent authority Eberhard Lämmert: "Er warf Hitler aus einem nachgerade unbändigen Widerwillen gegen die Demokratie ein noch zu hohes Maß an 'parlamentarischwestlichem Taktieren' vor und forderte statt dessen die kompromißlose Gewaltnahme im Staat" ("Beherrschte Prosa: Poetische Lizenzen in Deutschland zwischen 1933 und 1945," *Neue Rundschau* 86, no. 3 [1975]: 415).

3. By F. C. Weiskopf, *Unter fremden Himmeln*, p. 16. Werfel's ideological position in the thirties was representative of many European intellectuals. They were fascinated by the idea of fascism, but Hitler's tactics and the boorishness of many of his followers repelled them.

Chapter 8

1. Detailed and documented evidence that the United States government for more than a decade dragged its feet in this matter, and only belatedly made a genuine effort to rescue some of Hitler's victims, is presented by Arthur D. Morse in *While Six Million Died*.

2. The observations on Broch's *The Sleepwalkers* are based mainly on Theodore Ziolkowski, *Hermann Broch* (New York: Columbia University Press, 1964), p. 12.

3. At the time, alleged fascist traits in the Roosevelt administration were not infrequently pointed out by its opponents. In the intervening years that aspect of the New Deal has largely been forgotten, but recent

historical research has indicated that there was indeed a marked affinity between the methods and tactics employed by the American and German governments to cope with the political, social, and economic consequences of the Great Depression. The correspondence extended to the personal styles of the respective leaders. A detailed and carefully documented analysis of the similarities can be found in John A. Garraty, "The New Deal, National Socialism, and the Great Depression," *American Historical Review* 78 (1973): 907–44.

4. This statement and the following case histories are largely based on the extensive and well-documented observations of Joachim Radkau in *Die deutsche Emigration in den USA*, pp. 34–48 et passim.

5. In 1954, before McCarthy's fall, Schlamm contributed the prologue to William F. Buckley, Jr., and L. Brent Bozell, *McCarthy and His Enemies: The Record and Its Meaning* (Chicago: Henry Regnery, 1954). When the senator died, Schlamm wrote what has been characterized as "an emotional tribute" to him in the *National Review*. In the obituary, McCarthy was described as a man of "innocence" annihilated by the "hound-dogs of malice." See W. A. Swanberg, *Luce and His Empire*, p. 484.

6. Obviously the idea that the Social Democrats were willing to accept the Anschluß still arouses great and acrimonious passion and is vehemently denied by many. However, the cogent and well-documented argument in favor of this view presented by Franz Goldner (*Die Österreichische Emigration 1938 bis 1945*, pp. 149f) has so far elicited much hostile criticism, but no equally persuasive rebuttal.

Chapter 9

1. Like many other things about Bertolt Brecht, his command of English has been the subject of widely divergent views. The judgment expressed in the text that Brecht's grasp of the language was very imperfect is consistent with his own repeated assertions to that effect. Most established commentators accept his self-evaluation in this regard. See for instance Frederic Ewen, *Bertolt Brecht: His Life, His Art, and His Times* (New York: Citadel Press, 1967), p. 386.

Chapter 11

1. On the lack of resonance of the antifascist exile literature in postwar Germany, see Frank Trommler, "Emigration und Nachkriegs-

literatur," in *Exil und innere Emigration;* also Manfred Durzak, "Deutschsprachige Exilliteratur: Vom moralischen Zeugnis zum literarischen Dokument," in *Die Deutsche Exilliteratur 1933–1945*. The irrepressible Gottfried Benn in 1946 complained that the returning exiles were trying to push their pre-1933 ideas down the people's throats ("Nun kommen die von auswärts zurück und versuchen, uns die ollen Kamellen bis 1932 und ihre neuhinzugekommenen Ressentiments in den Rachen zu stopfen"). See *Als der Krieg zu Ende war* (Stuttgart: E. Klett, 1973), p. 243.

Chapter 12

1. This point is made emphatically by Uwe Schweikert, "Öfter als die Schuhe die Länder wechselnd," *Neue Rundschau* 85, no. 3 (1974): 489–501.

2. The notion of political literature has been, and continues to be, the subject of much heated controversy. There is a broad consensus that all literature in reflecting reality also mirrors, however indirectly, its historical and political aspects. What distinguishes real political literature is an activistic element that transcends the subjective sphere with a desire for effective intervention in the course of history. See Wolfgang Mohr and Werner Kohlschmidt, "Politische Dichtung," in *Reallexikon der deutschen Literaturgeschichte* 3, no. 2/3. 2d ed. (Berlin: Walter de Gruyter, 1966/7), p. 159. Mohr and Kohlschmidt also comment on the peculiar difficulties of judging political literature on its aesthetic merits. While it may be impossible to generalize, informed critical opinion has traditionally tended toward skepticism concerning the possibility of combining creative excellence and ideological activism. The prevailing scholarly view has been summed up in the formulation that literature that seeks to influence the political or cultural historical situation directly, "rarely achieves timeless or artistic-poetic value" ("selten überzeitlichen oder künstlerisch-dichterischen Wert erreicht") (Gero von Wilpert, *Sachwörterbuch der Literatur* [Stuttgart: Kröner, 1955], p. 432). The matter came to a head again in late 1966 when the eminent Swiss literary scholar Emil Staiger attacked the then prevailing view that revolutionary propaganda was the only viable and worthwhile form of writing. Staiger's criticism provoked massive attacks on his position and personality. Although much dust was raised in the following months, in the end the "Zurich Literature-Fight," as the altercation

came to be known, brought the basic dispute no closer to an objectively acceptable solution.

3. Feuchtwanger's problems with the German language have been described by Hans Mayer in "Lion Feuchtwanger oder die Folgen des Exils," *Neue Rundschau* 76, no. 1 (1965): 120–29. The discussion of Brecht and Thomas Mann and their respective modes of stylization largely follows the observations of Joachim Radkau, *Die deutsche Emigration in den USA*, pp. 113f. Radkau also draws a convincing parallel between these authors and another superlative stylist, Franz Kafka, who lived outside the German-speaking realm in Prague. Some aspects and ramifications of the language problem are considered, with reference also to other writers, by Egbert Krispyn, "Exil als Lebensform," in *Exil und Innere Emigration II*. Günther Anders deals with the matter from an autobiographical perspective in "Der Emigrant," *Merkur* 16, no. 7 (1962): 601–22.

4. This at least is the generally accepted version of her escape. Although it has been challenged, authoritative opinion still credits the intervention of Lagerlöf and Swedish royalty with rescuing Nelly Sachs from the Nazis. See for instance Hans-Albert Walter, *Deutsche Exilliteratur 1933–1950: Bedrohung und Verfolgung bis 1933*, p. 248.

Selected Bibliography

The following listing is on the whole limited to studies of rather broad scope. It does not for instance include the numerous analyses of specific works of exile literature and the profiles of individual exile authors that have been published in various journals devoted to Germanic philology. The *German Quarterly* in particular has since the 1940s printed a considerable number of such articles. The reader with a specialized interest in the literary historical aspects of the topic will have no difficulty in supplementing the titles cited here. Standard reference sources like the annual bibliography volume of *PMLA* contain much information on the subject, and other bibliographical materials have from time to time been made available to interested individuals and institutions by the "Stockholmer Koordinationsstelle zur Erforschung der deutschsprachigen Exil-Literatur" at Stockholm University, Sweden.

To keep the list within reasonable proportions, no primary exile literature has been included. Sternfeld and Tiedemann's *Deutsche Exil-Literatur 1933–1945* contains an extensive though not exhaustive survey of those writers and works that can be regarded as belonging to exile literature. Autobiographies have in only a few special cases been listed; they are in general unreliable as sources of information. Brief comments have been added to those titles that are not self-explanatory.

Als der Krieg zu Ende war. Literarisch-politische Publizistik 1945–1950: Ausstellungskatalog des Deutschen Literaturarchivs Marbach a. N. 1973. Stuttgart: E. Klett, 1973.
Anders, Günther. "Der Emigrant." *Merkur* 16, no. 7 (1962): 601–22. An autobiographical essay.

Andersch, Alfred. *Deutsche Literatur in der Entscheidung: Ein Beitrag zur Analyse der literarischen Situation.* Karlsruhe: Verlag Volk und Zeit, 1948. A charter for the Gruppe '47, with a critical appraisal of both the exile literature and the writing of the "inner emigration."

Benson, Frederick R. *Writers in Arms: The Literary Impact of the Spanish Civil War.* New York: New York University Press, 1967.

Berendsohn, Walter A. *Die humanistische Front: Einführung in die deutsche Emigranten-Literatur.* Part 1, *Von 1933 bis zum Kriegsausbruch 1939.* Zurich: Europa Verlag, 1946. Part 2, *Vom Kriegsausbruch 1939 bis Ende 1946.* Worms: Verlag Georg Heintz, 1976.

————. "Emigranten-Literatur 1933–1947." In *Reallexikon der deutschen Literaturgeschichte.* Vol. 1. Edited by W. Kohlschmidt and W. Mohr. 2d ed. Berlin: Walter de Gruyter, 1958.

Berthold, Werner, and Wilhelmi, Christa, eds. *Exil-Literatur 1933–1945: Eine Ausstellung aus Beständen der Deutschen Bibliothek, Frankfurt/Main.* Frankfurt am Main: Buchhändlervereinigung, 1966.

Boyers, Robert, ed. *The Legacy of the German Refugee Intellectuals.* 2d ed. New York: Schocken Books, 1972.

Bracher, Karl D. *Die deutsche Diktatur: Entstehung, Struktur, Folgen des Nationalsozialismus.* Cologne and Berlin: Kiepenheuer and Witsch, 1969.

Brenner, Hildegard. "Deutsche Literatur im Exil 1933–1947." In *Handbuch der deutschen Gegenwartsliteratur,* edited by Hermann Kunisch. Munich: Nymphenburger Verlagshandlung, 1965.

————. *Die Kunstpolitik des Nationalsozialismus.* Reinbek: Rowohlt, 1963. (Rowohlts Deutsche Enzyklopädie 167/68).

Cazden, Robert E. *German Exile Literature in America 1933–1950: A History of the Free German Press and Book Trade.* Chicago: American Library Association, 1970.

Crawford, William R., ed. *The Cultural Migration: The European Scholar in America.* Philadelphia: University of Pennsylvania Press, 1953.

Demetz, Peter. *Postwar German Literature: A Critical Introduction.* New York: Pegasus, 1970.

Döblin, Alfred. "Die deutsche Literatur im Ausland seit 1933." *Aufsätze zur Literatur.* Olten: Walter, 1963.

Doenitz, Karl. *Memoirs: Ten Years and Twenty Days.* 1959; rpt. New York: Leisure Books, [1974].

Drews, Richard, and Kantorowicz, Alfred, eds. *Verboten und verbrannt: deutsche Literatur zwölf Jahre unterdrückt.* Berlin: H. Ullstein, 1947.

Durzak, Manfred, ed. *Die Deutsche Exilliteratur 1933–1945.* Stuttgart:

Reclam, 1973. Part 1 contains brief surveys of the "exile situation" in the major host countries, and part 2 consists of essays on a number of individual figures.

Edinger, Lewis J. *German Exile Politics*. Berkeley: University of California Press, 1956.

Fest, Joachim C. *The Face of the Third Reich: Portraits of the Nazi Leadership*. Translated by Michael Bullock. New York: Pantheon, 1970.

Fetscher, Iring. "Bertolt Brecht und Amerika." In *The Legacy of the German Refugee Intellectuals*, edited by Robert Boyers. New York: Schocken Books, 1972.

Feuchtwanger, Lion. "Die Arbeitsprobleme des Schriftstellers im Exil." *Sinn und Form* 6, no. 3 (1954): 384ff.

——— *Unholdes Frankreich*. Mexico: Libro Libre, 1942. A personal memoir about the French internment camps.

Fischer, Ernst. *Erinnerungen und Reflexionen*. Reinbek: Rowohlt, 1969. An unorthodox Marxist's reminiscences, including the rise of Nazism and exile in the USSR.

Frei, Bruno. "Die deutsche antifaschistische literarische Emigration in Prag 1933–1936." In *Weltfreunde: Konferenz über die Prager deutsche Literatur*, edited by Eduard Goldstücker. Prague: Academia, 1967.

Friedrich, Otto. *Before the Deluge: A Portrait of Berlin in the 1920's*. New York: Harper and Row, 1972. New York: Avon Books, 1973.

Garraty, John A. "The New Deal, National Socialism, and the Great Depression." *American Historical Review* 78 (1973): 907–44.

Garten, Hugo F. "Main Trends in German Literature Today." *German Life and Letters*, New Series, vol. 1 (1947/48): 44–53.

Gay, Peter. *Weimar Culture: The Outsider as Insider*. New York: Harper and Row, 1968. An essayistic attempt to summarize the essence and history of the Weimar Republic.

Gilbert, G. M. *Nuremberg Diary*. 1947. Reprint. New York: New American Library, 1961. A record of the actions and statements of the prominent Nazis during the Nuremberg trials.

Gisevius, Hans B. *Der Anfang vom Ende: Wie es mit Wilhelm II begann*. Zurich: Droemer Knaur, 1971.

Goldner, Franz. *Die Österreichische Emigration 1938 bis 1945*. Vienna and Munich: Herold, 1972.

Goldstücker, Eduard, ed. *Weltfreunde: Konferenz über die Prager deutsche Literatur*. Prague: Academia, 1967.

Grimm, Reinhold. "Innere Emigration als Lebensform." In *Exil und*

Innere Emigration, edited by Reinhold Grimm and Jost Hermand. Frankfurt am Main: Athenäum, 1972.

————, and Hermand, Jost, eds. *Exil und innere Emigration*. Frankfurt am Main: Athenäum, 1972. A collection of papers. Those most relevant in the context of this study are cited under the names of the individual authors.

Grossberg, Mimi. *Österreichs literarische Emigration in den Vereinigten Staaten 1938*. Vienna: Europa Verlag, 1970.

Grosser, J. F. G., ed. *Die große Kontroverse: Ein Briefwechsel um Deutschland*. Hamburg, Geneva, and Paris: Nagel, 1963. Documents concerning the attempts of the "inner emigration" to discredit the exile writers after the end of the war.

Grossmann, Kurt R. *Emigration: Geschichte der Hitler-Flüchtlinge 1933–1945*. Frankfurt am Main: Europäische Verlagsanstalt, 1969.

————. *Ossietzky: Ein deutscher Patriot*. Frankfurt am Main: Suhrkamp, 1973.

Halfmann, Horst. "Literatur des Exils." *Neue Deutsche Literatur* 20 (1969): 183–86. A Marxist view.

Hamburger, Michael. *Zwischen den Sprachen*. Frankfurt am Main: Fischer, 1966. Observations on the linguistic and cultural situation of those who went into exile as children and as adults rediscovered their German heritage.

Häsler, Alfred A. *The Lifeboat is Full: Switzerland and the Refugees, 1933–1945*. New York: Funk and Wagnalls, 1969.

Hermand, Jost. "Schreiben in der Fremde: Gedanken zur deutschen Exilliteratur seit 1789." In *Exil und Innere Emigration*, edited by Reinhold Grimm and Jost Hermand. Frankfurt am Main: Athenäum, 1972.

Herzfelde, Wieland. "Erfahrungen im Exil zu Prag 1933–1938." In *Weltfreunde: Konferenz über die Prager deutsche Literatur*, edited by Eduard Goldstücker. Prague: Academia, 1967.

Hofe, Harold von. "Lion Feuchtwanger and America." In *Lion Feuchtwanger: The Man, His Ideas, and His Work*, edited by John M. Spalek. Los Angeles: Hennessey-Ingalls, 1972.

Hofer, Walther, ed. *Der Nationalsozialismus: Dokumente 1933–1945*. Frankfurt am Main: Fischer, 1957.

Hoffmann, Charles W. "Opposition und Innere Emigration: Zwei Aspekte des 'Anderen Deutschlands'." In *Exil und Innere Emigration II*, edited by Peter Uwe Hohendahl and Egon Schwarz. Frankfurt am Main: Athenäum, 1973.

Hohendahl, Peter U., and Schwarz, Egon, eds. *Exil und Innere Emigra-*

tion II. Frankfurt am Main: Athenäum, 1973. A collection of papers. Those most relevant in the context of this study are cited under the names of the individual authors.

Jacob, Hans. *Kind meiner Zeit: Lebenserinnerungen*. Cologne: Kiepenheuer and Witsch, 1962. Unreliable.

Jacobsen, Hans-Adolf, ed. *July 20, 1944. The German Opposition to Hitler as Viewed by Foreign Historians. An Anthology. Germans against Hitler*. Bonn: Press and Information Office of the Federal Government, 1969.

Jarmatz, Klaus. *Literatur im Exil*. Berlin: Dietz, 1966. A Marxist view.

Kamla, Thomas A. *Confrontations with Exile: Studies in the German Novel*. European University Papers, 1. German Language and Literature, vol. 137. Berne and Frankfurt am Main: Herbert Lang, 1975.

Kent, Donald P. *The Refugee Intellectual: The Americanization of the Immigrants of 1933–1941*. New York: Columbia University Press, 1953.

Kesten, Hermann, ed. *Deutsche Literatur im Exil: Briefe europäischer Autoren 1933–1949*. 1964. Reprint. Frankfurt am Main: Fischer, 1973.

————. *Meine Freunde die Poeten*. Vienna and Munich: Donau, 1953. Predominantly critical sketches of the author's literary colleagues in and out of exile.

Klieneberger, H. R. *The Christian Writers of the Inner Emigration*. The Hague and Paris: Mouton, 1968. A sectarian whitewash job.

Kobler, John. *Luce: His Time, Life and Fortune*. New York: Doubleday, 1968.

Krispyn, Egbert. "Exil als Lebensform." In *Exil und Innere Emigration II*, edited by Peter Uwe Hohendahl and Egon Schwarz. Frankfurt am Main: Athenäum, 1973.

Lämmert, Eberhard. "Beherrschte Prosa: Poetische Lizenzen in Deutschland zwischen 1933 und 1945." *Neue Rundschau* 86, no. 3 (1975): 404–21. Extremely valuable literary analysis of prose written in Nazi Germany.

Langer, Walter C. *The Mind of Adolf Hitler: The Secret Wartime Report*. New York: New American Library, 1973.

Larsen, Egon. "Deutsches Theater in London 1939–1945." *Deutsche Rundschau* 83 (April 1957): 378–83.

Lester, Conrad H. "Probleme der Österreichischen Literatur in der Emigration (Frankreich 1938–1940)." Reproduced from manuscript of lecture held at Vienna University on 16 May 1972.

Levin, Harry. "Literature and Exile." *Essays in Comparative Literature*.

Washington University Studies. St. Louis: Washington University, 1961. A general essay.

Lindt, Peter M. *Schriftsteller im Exil: Zwei Jahre deutsche literarische Sendung am Rundfunk in New York.* New York: Willard, 1944. Disappointingly superficial.

Link, Benjamin. "Die Österreichische Emigrantenpresse in den Subkulturen von New York City 1942 bis 1948." Ph.D. dissertation, University of Salzburg, 1972.

Lion, Ferdinand. "Zeitschriften unserer Zeit: *Der Neue Merkur—Mass und Wert.*" *Akzente* 10, no. 3 (1963): 34–40.

Lochner, Louis P., ed. *The Goebbels Diaries.* 1948. Reprint. New York: Universal-Award House, 1971.

Loewy, Ernst. *Literatur unterm Hakenkreuz: Das Dritte Reich und seine Dichtung. Eine Dokumentation.* Frankfurt am Main: Europäische Verlagsanstalt, 1966.

Lüth, Paul E. H. *Literatur als Geschichte: Deutsche Dichtung von 1885 bis 1947.* 2 vols. Wiesbaden: Limes, 1947.

Mahler-Werfel, Alma. *Mein Leben.* Frankfurt am Main: Fischer, 1963. Fascinating autobiography, particularly relevant in connection with Franz Werfel.

Manchester, William. *The Arms of Krupp 1587–1968.* Boston: Little, Brown, 1968. New York: Bantam Books, 1970. Especially informative on the subject of German heavy industry under the Nazis.

Mann, Erika and Mann, Klaus. *Escape to Life.* Boston: Houghton Mifflin, 1939. Autobiography by two prominent exiles.

Mann, Golo. *Deutsche Geschichte 1919–1945.* 1958. Reprint (Bücher des Wissens 387), Frankfurt am Main: Fischer, 1961.

———. "Deutsche Literatur im Exil." *Neue Rundschau* 79, no. 1 (1968): 38–49. Valuable survey.

———. "Die Brüder Mann und Bertolt Brecht: Einige Klarstellungen zu den eben veröffentlichten 'Arbeitsjournalen'." *Die Zeit*, 2 March 1973, pp. 9–10.

———. "Erinnerungen an meinen Bruder Klaus." *Neue Rundschau* 86, no. 3 (1975): 376–400.

Mann, Heinrich. *Ein Zeitalter wird besichtigt.* Stockholm: Bermann Fischer, 1946. Autobiographical survey of the Wilhelmian, Weimar, and Hitler eras.

Mann, Klaus. *The Turning Point.* New York: L. B. Fischer, 1942. Autobiographical work reflecting the author's earlier exile experiences. An expanded German version covering his later experiences in

wartime and postwar Europe appeared under the title *Der Wendepunkt*. Frankfurt am Main: Fischer, 1966.

Mann, Thomas. *Achtung Europa! Aufsätze zur Zeit*. New York and To-
ronto: Longmans Green, 1938.

―――. *Die Entstehung des Doktor Faustus*. 1949. Reprint. In *Doktor
Faustus/Die Entstehung des Doktor Faustus*. Frankfurt am Main: Fischer,
1967. Contains many observations on wartime and postwar problems
in the USA as they affected the most prominent exile.

―――. *Dieser Friede*. Stockholm: Bermann Fischer, 1938. A political
text.

―――. *The Coming Victory of Democracy*. New York: Knopf, 1938. A
political text.

Marcuse, Herbert. "Der Einfluß der deutschen Emigration auf das
amerikanische Geistesleben: Philosophie und Soziologie." *Jahrbuch
für Amerika-Studien* 10 (1965): 27–33.

Mayer, Hans. "Berlin 1947: Literarische Konfrontation der inneren und
äusseren Emigration." In *Exil und Innere Emigration*, edited by Reinhold Grimm and Jost Hermand. Frankfurt am Main: Athenäum,
1972.

―――. "Lion Feuchtwanger oder die Folgen des Exils." *Neue Rundschau* 76, no. 1 (1965): 120–29. Analyzes Feuchtwanger's changing
relation to the German language.

Mierendorff, Marta. "Deutsches Theater im Exil." *Die Deutsche Bühne* 5,
no. 1 (1961): 6–7.

Mohr, Oswald, ed. *Das Wort der Verfolgten*. Basel: Mundus Verlag,
1945. An anthology.

Morse, Arthur D. *While Six Million Died: A Chronicle of American
Apathy*. New York: Ace Publishing Corporation, n.d. Documented
description of "how America ducked chance after chance to save the
Jews."

Muschg, Walter. *Die Zerstörung der deutschen Literatur*. Berne: Francke,
1958. Essays on trends and figures in German literature and literary
scholarship.

Müssener, Helmut. *Die deutschsprachige Emigration in Schweden nach
1933: Ihre Geschichte und kulturelle Leistung*. Stockholm: University of
Stockholm, 1970.

―――. ed. *Protokoll des II. internationalen Symposiums zur Erforschung des
deutschsprachigen Exils nach 1933 in Kopenhagen 1972*. Stockholm:
University of Stockholm, 1972.

Neumann, Robert, and Koppel, Helga. *The Pictorial History of the Third
Reich*. New York: Bantam Books, 1962.

O'Connor, Richard. *The German Americans: An Informal History*. Boston: Little, Brown, 1968.

Osterle, Heinz D. "The Other Germany: Resistance to the Third Reich in German Literature." *German Quarterly* 44, no. 1 (1968): 1–22.

Pachter, Henry. "On Being an Exile: An Old-Timer's Personal and Political Memoir." In *The Legacy of the German Refugee Intellectuals*, edited by Robert Boyers. 2d ed. New York: Schocken Books, 1972.

Paetel, Karl O. "Die Presse des deutschen Exils 1933–1945." *Publizistik* 4, no. 4 (1959): 241–47.

Pfeiler, William K. *German Literature in Exile: The Concern of the Poets*. Lincoln: University of Nebraska Press, 1957. A pioneering effort, in some respects superseded by later studies.

Plessner, Monika. "Die deutsche 'University in Exile' in New York und ihr amerikanischer Gründer." *Frankfurter Hefte* 19 (March 1964): 181–86.

Poliakov, Leon, and Wulf, Josef. *Das Dritte Reich und seine Denker: Dokumente*. Berlin: Arani, 1959.

Radkau, Joachim. *Die deutsche Emigration in den USA: Ihr Einfluß auf die amerikanische Europapolitik 1933–45*. Studien zur modernen Geschichte, vol. 2. Düsseldorf: Bertelsmann, 1971. Probably the most important single source on the topic.

Regler, Gustav. *Das Ohr des Malchus: Eine Lebensgeschichte*. Cologne and Berlin: Kiepenheuer and Witsch, 1958. Important autobiography of an undogmatic Communist who later severed his ties with the Party.

———. *The Owl of Minerva*. New York: Farrar, Straus and Cudahy, 1960. Autobiographical novel.

Reich-Ranicki, Marcel. *Die Ungeliebten: Sieben Emigranten*. Opuscula 39. Pfullingen: Neske, 1968. Brief biographical sketches.

Remarque, Erich Maria. *Schatten im Paradies*. Munich: Droemer, 1971. Novel based on exile experiences.

Renn, Ludwig. *Warfare*. London: Faber and Faber, 1939. Observations of an ex-German army officer with radical leanings.

Rose, William. "German Literary Exiles in England." *German Life and Letters*, New Series, vol. 1 (1947/48): 175–85.

Sanders, Marion K. *Dorothy Thompson: A Legend in Her Time*. New York: Houghton Mifflin, 1973.

Schaber, Will, ed. *Aufbau-Rekonstruktion: Dokument einer Kultur im Exil*. New York and Cologne: Overlook Press, and Kiepenheuer and Witsch, 1972.

Scheer, Maximilian. *So war es in Paris*. Berlin: Verlag der Nation, 1964. On exile in prewar France.

Schlamm, Willi. *Diktatur der Lüge: Eine Abrechnung.* Zurich: Aufbruch, 1937. A spirited attack on fascism and Stalinism by a renegade Communist.

———. *This Second War of Independence.* New York: Dutton, 1940. A conservative exile's view on World War II.

Schröter, Klaus. "Der historische Roman des Exils und der inneren Emigration." In *Exil und Innere Emigration,* edited by Reinhold Grimm and Jost Hermand. Frankfurt am Main: Athenäum, 1972.

Schütz, William W. *Pens under the Swastika: A Study in Recent German Writing.* London: SCM Press, 1946.

Schwarz, Egon. "Was ist und zu welchem Ende studieren wir Exilliteratur?" In *Exil und Innere Emigration II,* edited by Peter Uwe Hohendahl and Egon Schwarz. Frankfurt am Main: Athenäum, 1973.

———, and Wegner, Matthias, eds. *Verbannung: Aufzeichnungen deutscher Schriftsteller im Exil.* Hamburg: H. Wegner, 1964. Valuable documentation.

Schweikert, Uwe. "Öfter als die Schuhe die Länder wechselnd: Notizen zur deutschen Exilliteratur, ihrer Rezeption und Erforschung." *Neue Rundschau* 85, no. 3 (1974): 489–501.

Sheean, Vincent. *Dorothy and Red.* London: Heinemann, 1964. On Dorothy Thompson.

Shirer, William L. *Berlin Diary: The Journal of a Foreign Correspondent 1934–1941.* New York: Popular Library, n.d.

———. *The Rise and Fall of the Third Reich: A History of Nazi Germany.* Greenwich: Fawcett Publications, n.d.

Soffke, Günther. *Deutsches Schrifttum im Exil (1933–1950): Ein Bestandverzeichnis.* Bonn: Bouvier, 1965.

Spalek, John M. "Ernst Tollers Vortragstätigkeit und seine Hilfsaktionen im Exil." In *Exil und Innere Emigration II,* edited by Peter Uwe Hohendahl and Egon Schwarz. Frankfurt am Main: Athenäum, 1973.

———, ed. *Lion Feuchtwanger: The Man, His Ideas and His Work.* Los Angeles: Hennessey and Ingalls, 1972.

Speer, Albert. *Inside the Third Reich.* New York: Macmillan, 1970. New York: Avon, 1971.

Stahlberger, Peter. *Der Zürcher Verleger Emil Oprecht und die deutsche politische Emigration 1933–1945.* Zurich, Vienna, and Frankfurt: Europa Verlag, 1970.

Stern, Guy. "Hinweise und Anregungen zur Erforschung der Exilliteratur." In *Exil und Innere Emigration II,* edited by Peter Uwe Hohendahl and Egon Schwarz, Frankfurt am Main: Athenäum, 1973.

Sternfeld, Wilhelm. "Die Emigrantenpresse." *Deutsche Rundschau* 77 (1950): 250–59.

———, and Tiedemann, Eva, eds. *Deutsche Exil-Literatur 1933–1945: Eine Bio-Bibliographie*. 2d ed. Heidelberg and Darmstadt: Lambert Schneider, 1970. An essential reference work.

Stourzh, Gerald. "Die deutschsprachige Emigration in den Vereinigten Staaten: Geschichtswissenschaft und Politische Wissenschaft." *Jahrbuch für Amerika-Studien* 10 (1965): 59–77.

Strothmann, Dietrich. *Nationalsozialistische Literaturpolitik: Ein Beitrag zur Publizistik im Dritten Reich*. 2d ed. Bonn: Bouvier, 1963.

Swanberg, W. A. *Luce and His Empire*. New York: Dell, 1973.

Trommler, Frank. "Emigration und Nachkriegsliteratur: Zum Problem der geschichtlichen Kontinuität." In *Exil und Innere Emigration*, edited by Reinhold Grimm and Jost Hermand. Frankfurt am Main: Athenäum, 1972.

Tucholsky, Kurt. *Ausgewählte Briefe 1913–1935*. Hamburg: Rowohlt, 1962.

Vasari, Emilio. *Dr. Otto Habsburg oder die Leidenschaft für Politik*. Vienna and Munich: Herold, 1972.

Vesely, Jiri. "Zur Geschichte einer Prager Emigrantenzeitschrift (Der Simplicius/Der Simpl)." In *Weltfreunde: Konferenz über die Prager deutsche Literatur*, edited by Eduard Goldstücker. Prague: Academia, 1967.

Wächter, Hans-Christof. *Theater im Exil: Sozialgeschichte des deutschen Exiltheaters 1933–1945*. Munich: Hanser, 1973.

Walter, Hans-Albert. *Deutsche Exilliteratur 1933–1950*. 10 vols. Darmstadt and Neuwied: Luchterhand. Vol. 1, *Bedrohung und Verfolgung bis 1933*, 1972. Vol. 2, *Asylpraxis und Lebensbedingungen in Europa*, 1972. Vol. 7, *Exilpresse I*, 1974. A valuable repository of facts, but their presentation is narrowly leftist.

Wegner, Matthias. *Exil und Literatur: Deutsche Schriftsteller im Ausland 1933–1945*. 2d ed. Frankfurt am Main: Athenäum, 1968. An early scholarly attempt at surveying the topic, still worth reading.

Wehdeking, Volker C. *Der Nullpunkt: Über die Konstituierung der deutschen Nachkriegsliteratur, 1945–1948, in den amerikanischen Kriegsgefangenenlagern*. Stuttgart: Metzler, 1971. Important study.

Weisenborn, Günther. *Der lautlose Aufstand: Bericht über die Widerstandsbewegung des deutschen Volkes 1933–1945*. Hamburg: Rowohlt, 1953.

Weiskopf, Franz C. *Unter fremden Himmeln: Ein Abriß der deutschen*

Literatur im Exil 1933–1947. Mit einem Anhang von Textproben aus Werken exilierter Schriftsteller. Berlin: Dietz, 1947. One of the first comprehensive surveys. The author's Marxism does not detract from its value.

Weisstein, Ulrich. "Literaturkritik in deutschen Exil-Zeitschriften: Der Fall *Das Wort.*" In *Exil und Innere Emigration II*, edited by Peter Uwe Hohendahl and Egon Schwarz. Frankfurt am Main: Athenäum, 1973.

Wellek, Albert. "Der Einfluß der deutschen Emigration auf die Entwicklung der nordamerikanischen Psychologie." *Jahrbuch für Amerika-Studien* 10 (1965): 34–58.

White, Lyman C. *Three Hundred Thousand New Americans: The Epic of a Modern Immigrant-Aid Service.* New York: Harper and Brothers, 1957.

Wittlin, Jospeh. "Sorrow and Grandeur of Exile." *Polish Review* 2, no. 2/3 (1957): 99–111. General reflections.

Wulf, Josef. *Literatur und Dichtung im Dritten Reich: Eine Dokumentation.* 1963. Reprint. Reinbek bei Hamburg: Rowohlt, 1966.

Wyman, David S. *Paper Walls: America and the Refugee Crisis 1938–1941.* Amherst: University of Massachusetts Press, 1968.

Zentner, Kurt. *Illustrierte Geschichte des Widerstandes in Deutschland und Europa, 1933–1945.* Munich: Südwest Verlag, 1966.

Zuckmayer, Carl. *Als wär's ein Stück von mir.* 1967. Reprint. Frankfurt am Main: Fischer, 1969. Autobiography.

Index

Index